MY

WAY

FORWARD

MY

WAY

FORWARD

Turning Tragedy into Triumph

MOLEI WRIGHT

atmosphere press

DEDICATION

Dr. Spier, Dr. Puschak, Dr. Clary, Dr. Yarnell, Dr. Colbert-Falin, Dr. Brown, Dr. Buzan, Dr. Gerber, Ashley, Brooke, Courtney, Melissa, Nina, Leah, Wendy, Diane, Judy, Stephanie, Angela, Joan, Casey, Jen, June (my respiratory therapist), Vikki and Vivian (the front administration people who would check me in at Craig)

To all my therapists I've worked with. I've formed friendships with each of you and have taken away more than you know from each of them. You came into my life because it was your job to, but I truly consider myself lucky to have met you. You are the obvious silver lining in this whole ordeal. Without you it would be so much harder to find the good in this terribly dark time in my life.

To all my nurses I had. **I had two nurses a day and two CNAs a day, and that's just the protocol for the rehabilitation hospital I was at—I don't know the protocol for the three other hospitals I spent time at. I was at a total of four hospitals for a total of 151 days...I was only conscious for the last forty-three days. It's impossible for me to name every nurse that took care of me so if I missed your name, please know I'm sincerely sorry and I've overlooked you because of my comatose state I was in and not because of anything you did or didn't do! **Especially to the ones at Craig: it takes a special type of person to do the work you do—the dirty work or the "small" stuff (like personal hygiene compared to spinal surgery)...nonetheless, it's the *small stuff* that matters most to humanity and, arguably, makes the biggest impact on patients.

Ambyr, it was the little giggles you chose to share *with me, even though this was before I could communicate with words.* Hannah, it was the effort you made *after I was discharged from the hospital* and knowing I had zero recollection of you (because you were one of the ICU nurses at the first hospital I was in a coma in) that made such an impact on me. Rachel and Darcy, you brought a sense of connection to me when I was an outsider in my own life because you knew me from outside the hospital. Thank you for making me feel welcome and included despite my reluctance to accept the reality.

And to Brittany and Henry. Thank you for saving mine and Jeremy's lives that night. Thank you for stopping and putting your life in danger all to help me; a stranger you didn't even know. I'm so thankful that you just so happened to be traveling on the same road at just the right time and above that, you decided to step up and take action. Not only that, but you took the effort to reach out and find me after the initial accident and we've since formed a forever friendship.

You, both, have welcomed Jeremy and I into your lives as well as your families. I will forever have a deep gratitude for you two. I love you.

And for Patrick. My BFFAE (best friend forever and ever)

PREFACE

Writing this book was one of the hardest things I've ever done but it gave me so much more. It gave me a way to unpack my life and look at this accident as an outsider. I was able to look at hardships I went through because of it (like lost friendships and distressed family ties) and make sense of them. I was able to see, in the end, everything that happened—good or bad—happened with *my* say.

There were times when I started writing about a tumultuous time and it would take me days to recount the events that happened, not because of memory but because it was too hard for me to emotionally revisit the experience. Sharing memories would leave me longing for the way things used to be, back when I could send a quick text to a girlfriend because I just saw a funny commercial that reminded me of an inside joke we shared from our college days, or daily phone calls I would have with my mom. I hadn't mentally prepared myself for this rush of nostalgia so without a proper defense mechanism, I'd fall into a stupor of me binge watching episodes of *Friends*. *Friends* can always make me laugh, and I've seen every episode enough times to know each one by memory. Watching it is truly a mindless event for me.

Aside from the painful memories that arose with the writing of this book, it also pointed out to me that I've felt a struggle with individuality after the accident. Not so much self-identity but more so just the fact that I *am* an individual…with my own feelings and thoughts, and I deserve happiness just like all people do. I think since Jeremy has been by my side through it all, it was easy for people to just sort of combine us into one person. We were "Molei and Jeremy"…not one person named Molei and another person named Jeremy. If Jeremy was upset with something Molei must be upset too. Or, more frustratingly with my family specifically, if I voiced an opposing opinion it must be because Jeremy was whispering that in my ear to give me that opinion; there's no way I was capable of having my own thoughts and opinions for myself. It also happened in the hospital. After waking up from my coma, doctors and nurses warned my family I *may* be different and not to be surprised or taken back if I was. We've all heard stories of the person who survives a brain injury but they're a completely different person because of it. That wasn't the case for me, and even if it was—even if I woke up a completely different person who got mad and angry easily—it shouldn't serve to invalidate any of my emotions. There was one time in the hospital when a nurse didn't get there in time to help me use the bathroom. (This was before I could get to the bathroom on my own so I needed to press a button that would call a nurse to come and assist me.) I had pushed the button, summoning a nurse, but the nurse never came. I sat there clenching my legs anxiously waiting for her arrival. With my eyes closed, all my focus was on holding everything up. As I sat there my back got a little straighter, my shoulders were held up close to my ears (as if the placement of my shoulders has anything to do with my urination.) Logic held no importance at this point; in my mind, pee goes down so I needed to hold everything *up*. Seconds turned into minutes and minutes turned to hours. HOURS...*four to be exact*. The nurse didn't come until my brother (who was visiting me at that time) went out to the hall to go flag a nurse down. My brother was sitting at the edge of the bed with me when my eyes started to water. (Side note: my eyes always tear up when I pee...I don't know why but it has *always* been this way. To me, when you pee, your eyes water.) He asked, "Are you crying? Are you ok? Are you in pain?" to which I had to answer him with the painful truth that I had just peed myself. When the nurse did finally, come in, she said in that way you naively ask an obvious question that you already know the answer to, "Oh no! Did we have an accident?" My mom had just walked into the room and was unaware of the situation when she asked the nurse what was going on. At this point, I'm angry. I'm mad because my page went unanswered, I'm embarrassed because I just peed myself in front of my younger brother and frankly, I'm annoyed that I was being talked to like a child by the nurse. So I answered in what could only be taken as a fit of anger in my quieted voice, "*WE* DIDN'T PEE...*I* PEED!" And the next part I don't think I said (because I didn't have the breath control to say this many words) but I can assure you I was thinking it: *And this was no accident. If you came when I first paged four hours ago, I wouldn't be in this situation!* After the nurse took me to the bathroom and helped me clean myself up, she wheeled me back to bed. I can only assume I had daggers shooting out of my eyes and I was flushed with rage because as the nurse was transferring me back into bed my mom was overly polite as to make up for my lack of gratitude. As the nurse left I heard my mom apologize again at the door and the nurse say, "Oh no, it's fine. We're trained professionals to deal with brain injured patients. Patients getting angry is part of the job". That's true; they are trained to know how to deal with fits of rage or outbursts of anger, but this wasn't one of those moments. This was a twenty-nine-year-old woman being embarrassed by peeing in her own pants, *in front of her younger brother*. I knew I did not want to do that...pee in my pants. I knew peeing in my pants is an embarrassing act and I wanted to avoid the aftermath. Knowing this was the exact situation I was trying to avoid, and I did everything in *my* power to avoid it yet it wasn't avoidable—not because of a lack on any of *my efforts,* but a lack on someone else's effort. *That* was frustrating to me. Even thinking back on it: yeah it was frustrating then, but it infuriates me now. This story only serves to accentuate the importance of keeping individuality...humanity...respect, really. I understand the brain is a complex organ that's capable of an array of different levels of recovery. But just because I now have a brain injury, it shouldn't put me in a box. You're not allowed to tell me I'm mad because of my brain injury and not because I was lying in my own bodily excrement. I know that everything said and done to me was out of compassion. The nurse coming in and childishly asking me if I had an accident wasn't done to belittle or embarrass me, it was intended to do the exact opposite. Unfortunately, it did just that because I was already embarrassed and belittled.

What I'm able to see now, but didn't see at the time, comes out of my mindfulness work accomplished in outpatient care at Craig. A lot of frustrations of mine come from people making assumptions about me because I'm a TBI patient. In the previous example—I was presumed to be mad because of my TBI and *not* because a nurse failed to help me to the toilet in time. My financials—my money is locked up in a trust because of the assumption that brain injured people can't handle their own money. I went to court and passionately defended my rights only to have the judge say she couldn't grant me my rights because of the injuries I sustained. Those are just two examples because I don't want to bore you with a thousand-page book filled with examples of how my individuality was stripped from me with the diagnosis of a TBI. As aggravating as these examples are, leaving me with a festering pot of anger, what I'm able to acknowledge now is that simmering pot of frustration and anger does nothing for me. What are my choices: to scream and yell at the nurse angrily announcing that I'm not the typical TBI patient? Right—that's like screaming you're quiet…good luck with that. (I hope you can see my eye rolls right now) Was I going to beg and plead 'til I was crying to the judge to give me full access to *my* money? I highly doubt that would solidify my argument of financial and emotional intelligence…a girl begging for money while mascara runs down her face. I had to find peace in the reality, and sadly that reality is that sometimes people just can't see past the TBI. And that's their loss, not mine.

In order to come to that conclusion, I had to do a lot of self work and become very confident in my values and morals. I had to become ok with walking away from the situation. I can make my claim and once it's out there my job is done. I can't force the other person to believe it; they can take it or leave it. The hard part for me was to be ok with myself if they choose to leave it. I'll use my financials as an example again. I made my claim that I was of able consciousness to handle my own money, but the judge didn't take it. Because of that choice, I'm left with a trust that locks my money up. That was four years ago; I could've wasted countless hours complaining and wishing it went my way but what good would that do? That wasn't going to change the outcome. Instead, I've opened a separate bank account and invested in different things to try and make my own money *outside* of the trust. In that four years, I didn't waste valuable time thinking of what *could have been*. I worked on making what I want for the future. If someone wants to look at me differently for having a TBI, then so be it. I can only be me. And that's a tutor at the elementary school teaching kids how to read, it's a friend who will listen to any issue on your mind and will help you come up with a solution, it's someone who will cook you dinner but I probably don't have a recipe for it, it's a slightly obsessed dog lover who has *never* been good with navigational direction. I'm a proud TBI survivor who's finding my way forward.

CHAPTER ONE-
INTRODUCTION

The near-fatal accident I was in does not define who I am. I am not *just* a traumatic brain injury (TBI) patient. My life is not defined by those six long months spent in the hospital. But many formative events happened as a result of the accident that have formed me into who I am today.

I choose to write my story now, four and a half years post-accident, because it's taken this long for me to feel proud of telling it. I choose to take the realities (many of which are hardships) and turn them into successes. I'm sure my story could have been just another mishap. The kind of experience you only hear about on the news—about a girl who had an unfortunate twist of fate and all the depressing events that follow—but I don't want that kind of story. I want one filled with happiness and hope. It took thirty-three years of living to really know myself; and it wasn't just the years that did it. It took a brain injury, lost friendships, broken family relationships, relearning how to do *everything,* enough tears to fill the Atlantic Ocean, and (lots of) therapy to get me to feel comfortable and accepting of who I am. If, four years ago, the ghost-of-Molei's-future came to current Molei to warn her not to get in the car that night, knowing what I know now—going through all the hardship and pain but gaining a true grasp on my values and morals—I'd get in the car. This is my story of how I found *my way forward*. Even in the darkest of times, there's a way forward…it just may not look the way you expected it to.

My name is Molei (pronounced Molly) Wright. I'm a thirty-two-…thirty-three-year-old female living a regular life. (I joke that since I was in a coma for one of my birthdays, that one doesn't count.) I live with my boyfriend, Jeremy, and together we have a dog, Jaxon. Jeremy "adopted" Jax who has stolen his heart in the five years we've been together. Jaxon has been with me for the past eleven years. If you're picturing an old, slow-moving, always-confused dog, you are sorely mistaken. He's the Benjamin Button of dogs—he's got more spry in him now than he did as a puppy. But enough about him, I'm sure he doesn't hold a candle to *your* dog, the cutest dog.

I'm just another regular millennial but I am a survivor of a near-death car accident that left me with a TBI, and the recovery has brought me lots of wisdom that I'm here to share.

Five years ago, if someone had asked me who I was, I would have answered: I'm Molei. I have a boyfriend, Jeremy (I love him, but I wouldn't tell you that since I haven't told him yet). I am a daughter of a quilt-loving mother and a BloKart enthusiast father. I am the goody-two-shoes younger sister to my older sister, and a reclusive but supportive older sister to my three younger siblings. I am very close to my parents—my mom is my best friend. I have a great group of girlfriends that I consider more like sisters. I know all girls say that, but this is true. We've stuck together through everything and remained close for twenty-plus years. I am living with a girlfriend in the trendy uptown district of Downtown Denver where everything is within walking distance of my apartment, including my job as a financial wholesaler where I work selling mutual funds. I like living so close to work because I've never liked driving; it's not *my* driving I worry about, it's the fact that I can't control how the other cars on the road will drive. *Too much uncertainty for my liking. I'm not going to gamble with my luck daily when the option of walking is right there.* Come sunshine or snow, I make the twelve-block walk daily. In the spring and summer months, I play volleyball on a co-ed, grass-league team. I walk that line of playing the sport seriously and for fun…I have the competitiveness of a professional athlete playing in the championship but the skill of a varsity player because that's exactly what I was; varsity captain is as far as my resume takes me—athletically that is. Academically is a different story. I've always taken academics very seriously. I blame it on my competitiveness; back in third grade we had a thing called Math Olympics, and you bet your ass I made sure to make the team. I also won the competition for designing the T-shirt but that's an accolade I'm just bragging about. I graduated high school with honors and went on to be the first one in my immediate family to attend college. I not only attended college, but I graduated with a Bachelor of Science degree in Biomedical Sciences. It was a major that you had to be accepted into and maintain a certain GPA to earn your degree. Upon graduating in 2010, I went on to work countless jobs in the medical field but since I didn't have an MD or nursing degree, I found the only work I was qualified for was administrative, front-office work.

So, in 2014 I made the decision of a lifetime (at that time) to switch careers from the medical field to the financial field. Once I got a foot in the door I was able to work my way up the "corporate ladder" and earn my Series 6 (a license required to sell financial securities) to earn a job as an internal wholesaler, which was a step up from the administrative work I was doing as a scheduler.

That's who I was five years ago. Now, that has all changed. And if you ask me, it was the accident that caused all the change. I no longer work at my job as an internal wholesaler selling mutual funds—because the TBI has made it close to impossible to ever work again. I'm no longer on my volleyball team—because I couldn't even stand after waking up from the coma, let alone play volleyball. I'm no longer friends with many of my friends, because we had a falling out for some reason. I say it was because of this accident but when I asked one of my girlfriends, she said she doesn't think it's the accident. She said, "As with all friendships you evolve into your own person with your own life." But if you ask me, I don't buy it. That's exactly what a friendship is: finding companionship and company in someone else while still maintaining your own separate lives. I had that for twenty-plus years with many girls. If the tables were turned and one of my friends were severely hurt and left bedridden at her parents', I would make the extra effort to go visit her and maintain that friendship. But it wasn't one of my friends who got severely hurt in the accident; they weren't the ones left bedridden; it was me...*I* got hurt in an accident. I'm not upset about the fact that I was the one to get hurt— no one can control that, that's life—I'm more upset with how that was handled. I'm not sure who first said it, but a quote I've come to live by goes something like this, "You can't control what will happen, but you **can** control how you react to it." I'm let down by how this all panned out— I'm upset and disappointed that these friendships just crumbled and no longer existed when this accident abruptly came barging through the friendships' door. I had to come to the decision to close that door and move on; however, it's not *locked*. I'll always save space in my heart for my previous friendships so if someone decides to try and reignite that burnt-out flame, I will gladly and excitedly try to help; nothing would make me happier. I just can't keep getting my hopes up and being the only one to put in the effort. It's emotionally exhausting and damaging. It started to feel like trying to start a fire underwater; it just can't be done.

I'm no longer best friends with my mom, and as a matter of fact, each one of my relationships with each of my immediate family members was hurt, but we're working on repairing them. I have high, realistic hopes that my strong family relationships will come back.

The accident and TBI resulted in me grappling with this whole new life of mine and learning lesson after lesson. Lessons that are specific to my new life as a disabled person, and more general life lessons pertaining to my friends, family, and relationships. I've also discovered a new passion: teaching kids how to read. This passion has given me a calling and reason for being. Viktor Frankl says in his book *Man's Search for Meaning* that most people think about one, broad meaning for life. But he thinks the meaning can change from time to time to be more specific in the current situation. I believe that. I don't think when I was born, or even five years ago, helping kids with reading was my purpose. But today; today it gives me meaning in life.

I spent close to six months in three different hospitals. After coming home from the final hospital, I found myself feeling thankful for anything I had. There would be mornings I'd be leaning back as my mom administered my daily meds through a tube hanging out of my stomach (before I learned how to swallow and eat again), and I remember thinking, *Man, I'm so grateful I can be sitting on my couch rather than a hospital bed.* I have gratitude for just about everything in my life which has, in turn, made me into a pretty positive person. I can always find the silver lining in an event, which I'm sure can be annoying at times (I'm thinking of the character of Phoebe's painfully positive boyfriend, played by Alec Baldwin on *Friends*.)

I don't want to come off like that, which is why I tell myself to allow negative thoughts to come in or be said, acknowledge them and the emotions that come alongside of them, and then think of a way to rectify it. Basically, I find a way to put myself to work; or else, knowing me, I'll sit and ruminate on the negative thoughts and the negative emotions that come with them. My positive outlook on life is a product of my selfishness. I don't like being sad, mad, or depressed, and being negative only leads me to those emotions. Therefore, I just choose to be positive so I can avoid those negative emotions. Easy.

Another trait worth mentioning is my determination. However, it's not one that I noticed specifically after the accident. Rather, my determination was accentuated by the events that came as a result of the accident. For example, the car crash robbed me of my ability to walk, so

I had to relearn once I awoke from my coma and got well enough to participate in physical therapy. Craig Hospital is a rehabilitation hospital for spinal cord and brain injuries so there are many patients who suffer injuries that cause paralysis. Walking isn't an option. The Craig staff help these patients and teach them how to live in their new life of no walking.

When I woke up from my coma, walking wasn't guaranteed. I didn't have doctors promising me I'll walk again. My doctor, Dr. Spier, told me, "I don't know what, for certain, is possible in your recovery. But I promise, I won't limit you…meaning, if you want to walk again, I will help you get the therapy needed." This is where my determination came in. I was afforded the help I needed to reach my goal, but without my determination, I wouldn't be where I am today. There were plenty of times I could have given up after my failed attempts, but I wouldn't let myself. Sure, there were times when I would get angry or sad but I specifically remember saying to myself, *Ok Mol, you're allowed to wallow in self-pity for one hour. Then after that, that's it. It's back to work!* I'm so very grateful I was blessed with that outlook. I don't know why but quitting was just never an option. It wasn't even a thought.

My outlook on life is a direct result of the experiences I endure in the new life I'm living. I look at my injuries and the disabilities that come with it as a personal injustice. Just because I was in a terrible accident and suffered near-fatal injuries doesn't mean I should be discounted or looked on as a lesser person. It may mean it will be more of a challenge for me to live, but if I'm willing to face those challenges head-on, and prove myself capable of overcoming them, no one should be able to tell me I can't. Anyone who says I can't, I'm out to prove wrong.

From the moment I woke up from the coma, the words "you can't" have been an *everyday* occurrence. If someone tells me, "Molei, you can't do that…." and I feel I can do it, then my new goal is to do that thing even if it's just to spite them. However, I've always been a rule-follower so this was a difficult adjustment to become comfortable with. Usually if someone told me I can't…I didn't. Lifeguards told me, "No running by the pool," so walking it was. The sign said exit only, so I would enter using the other door. The light was red, so I stopped. I lived my life by rules; no running in the hallways, no talking in the movie theatre, say your please's and thank you's. I was a rule follower. I still am, but if anything, if someone tells me I can't, I take it with a grain of salt; whereas before, if someone told me I couldn't, I would take it more as fact.

It started in the hospital. The nurses told me I couldn't sleep with the walls unlocked and open on my bed. And I can understand that; a main concern was falling out of bed. I had fallen before and the sole reason I was in a bed that had walls was to keep me in—to keep me from falling. There were plenty of rules in the hospital: no trying to move or even sit up on your own, no wheeling around without a Posey belt[1], ALWAYS have your seatbelt on in the wheelchair, no guests out of visiting hours, no showing up late to therapies…you name it, there was probably a rule for it. But it didn't bother me. The rules are there *for* us, the patients in the hospital. I've always been stubborn though. My doctors and nurses learned that quickly. My main neurologist at Craig Hospital was always honest with

---

[1] A padded restraint belt intended for "patients who have the tendency to slide forward." (Posey.com)

me and told me my prognosis in each situation. Then I would say, "With all due respect, I'm going to prove you wrong!" He replied, "I look forward to you proving me wrong; I expect nothing less of you. I support you 100%!"

I didn't realize how much I would rely on those words of encouragement especially since my world was quickly inundated with, "No, you can't," or "Molei, you just can't do that..." When I was first discharged from the hospital and I was living at my mom's house, I was in a wheelchair. However, I was still going to physical therapy at Craig and learning how to walk. There was a time I used a walker as a transition from using a wheelchair to walking. Simple decisions such as using my wheelchair to get from my room to the family room were met with fraught debate. My mom felt it was safer for me to use the wheelchair, but, in my mind, I questioned how I was ever going to progress to walking if I used my wheelchair at all times. She said, "Molei, you *can't* use the walker..." I'm sure she meant I couldn't use the walker for safety reasons and not because of my physical capabilities, but I heard it as I'm not capable of using the walker. Anytime someone says I can't do something, it's an automatic challenge to me. Of course, if someone says I can't sprout wings and fly, I know to take that as fact...no one can grow wings and fly. But, if you're telling me I can't do something you can do...well, challenge accepted, my friend.

Of course, there are things I can't do, for example, I can't move my 100-pound treadmill, but rest assured I tried. I had to have my boyfriend come help get me unstuck and pull the box off of me when I found myself trapped underneath it. The point is, I'm the one who determined I couldn't move it for myself; I would not

11

accept someone else telling me I couldn't.

I have my own house that I live in with my boyfriend, Jeremy, and my dog, Jaxon. In that aspect I like to think that's where my life doesn't differ from the next early-thirties woman. I cook dinners for us and clean up. (I'm realizing how fifties-housewife that must sound but it's really not...I promise.) When I was first discharged from the hospital and living at my parents' house, I was basically a good-for-nothing, waste-of-space, living-at-home millennial. I would eat *someone else's* food, sleep on *someone else's* bed, and watch *someone else's* TV on *someone else's* couch. I didn't even clean up after myself because it wasn't expected of me. A few months into living at my parents', I remember a challenge of mine was to fold my laundry and to do light chores I could do without putting myself in danger. (If I sat while I folded clothes I could avoid falling. But moving clothes from the washer to dryer involved standing which could lead to a fall) I'm not lying or overexaggerating when I say this brain injury took everything away from me and pushed me back to start. I was forced to relearn the basics. I was like a child learning to do and take on basic responsibilities, but I had the unique perception of looking at my tasks, like folding laundry, as therapy instead of the dreaded chore to earn my playtime outside or my sleepovers with friends on the weekend. I now have the luxury of dreading those chores because I actually have enough abilities to be expected to use them. Cooking is a different story, though. I don't dread it like I used to. I think my old perspective of *why would anyone cook when there are restaurants?* was because I never gave cooking a good try. Cooking became my daily occupational therapy (OT), so it gave me a reason to do it, and I actually came to like it. In the beginning I would follow the recipes and instructions to a T. If the recipe called for a cup of water I would grab out the measuring cup and make sure the water line hit right at the one-cup line—if it was slightly higher I would dump out the excess and re-measure to achieve the exactness I desired. I crossed all T's and dotted all i's. Now that I've cooked so many different recipes I can "eyeball" the needed amount. I've even gotten so cocky with my skills that I can taste what spices needs to be added. But it's that confidence or "eyeballing" skill that is exactly why you won't get a good recipe from me. My recipes include "a dash of salt" or a "bowl of water" or a "heap of spinach"... all very subjective measurements. (That's why I just do the cooking.)

One aspect of mine that does make me different is my recovery from my TBI. It's something that I think about *often* and randomly and I'm, truly, so grateful that I've been able to recover so well. My therapies and involvement in different groups at Craig Hospital have introduced me to so many TBI survivors whose recoveries range in all different levels. Some are way better off than me and living their independent lives with their careers, while others aren't as fortunate and require a caregiver, often in the form of a parent or spouse. Of course there are things I wish I could do; I wish I could talk better, I wish I could run, I wish my balance wasn't messed up so badly; but there are also times when I think of how much worse things could have been, and those times are much more often than the others. There are plenty of patients who suffer an injury causing paralysis and can no longer walk or use their arms. I'm no longer in a wheelchair and was able to relearn how to walk. Not only can I walk on my own but I got my driver's license back. After many grueling therapies that tested my peripheral sight and my reaction time, and prepared me for the six-hour driving test, I successfully showed the doctors I could drive safely. It was *much* more comprehensive than the test I took at the DMV at sixteen, but nonetheless, I took it and passed it. I was able to buy a car with my settlement money. I can now drive myself around and I'm no longer dependent on NEMTs (non-emergency medical transportation) or public transportation/Ubers. I was also able to buy my own house where I can live without my parents. I can cook my own meals, clean my own messes and fix (or call a handyman to fix) any house maintenance required.

One final thing I can say about myself is that I'm very intentional now. That is something that has come to fruition because of the accident. One of the classes I was assigned to as part of my therapies at Craig Hospital was called "Mindfulness." That's where I learned how to meditate and the benefits that come with meditating and being mindful. It's something I've carried into my life after my time at Craig came to a close.

It wasn't until an adaptive yoga class I took that I realized just how intentional I was. Our lesson that day was about being intentional, so as an example, we practiced some intentional eating with a raisin. It took a lot longer because we were taking our time to notice the different aspects of the raisin in our mouths. (What's the texture like? Do we like that? Why or why not? What about the taste? Is it more of a sour taste or sweet?) The point of the exercise was to pick a simple task we do daily without thinking (like eating) and slow it down to bring every little step into detail…to make it intentional. What was done as an exercise to point out the ease and automation done in an every-day task, like eating, didn't apply to me or my life anymore because of the accident. The accident robbed me of any normalcy or automatic actions and because of this, I didn't come to the same conclusion as others in the class came to—that the action of eating a raisin is so easy it had become unintentional. The actions weren't thoughtless or automatic to me because I had just relearned how to do them. I performed all these tasks with thought because I *had* to; I just learned how to do it. Eating is a perfect example. I know softer things take less effort than chewy things. Mashed potatoes are much easier than celery, which is super stringy and chewy at the end of the bite. I know crunchier things tend to be easier than something really smooth and flat like a piece of spinach. I know the thinner the liquid, the harder to swallow—which is why I order milkshakes when possible when I'm out for a drink with friends.

Eating has become very intentional for me, but other things have as well. Like getting dressed in the morning. I know that since I have limited range of motion in my left arm, in order to put on a shirt I need to start with the left arm because when my head is in the shirt, my right arm has to move to find the arm hole. When I'm taking it off, it's the opposite. Start with the right arm so at the end I can slide the T-shirt off of the immobilized left arm. When I'm putting my pants on, I know to start with the right leg because my right side is stronger, which makes it better at balancing, so I can spend longer amounts of time on one foot when it's my right foot. (That's when I challenge myself to put pants on while standing up.)

My speech therapist taught me to think about which words are important in what I am saying and the shortest way to say it because my breath control is all messed up from having a paralyzed vocal cord. (Example: Say, "I need the remote." Don't say, "Can you please pass the remote?"—four words versus six.)

My days became filled with different therapies teaching me tricks to help me do everyday things more easily...like make sure you have important key words in the beginning of your sentence. Or when walking up steps, be sure to always start the step with your stronger side. Going down steps, start with your weaker side.

You would be surprised at how much reason and thinking goes into everything I do. This accident has forced me to be intentional. A favorite quote of mine is from L. R. Knost.

> "Do not be dismayed by the brokenness of the world. All things break. And all things can be mended. Not with time, as they say, but with intention. So go. Love intentionally, extravagantly, unconditionally. The broken world waits in darkness for the light that is you."

CHAPTER TWO-
THE ACCIDENT

On January 29, 2016, at approximately 2030 hours, I, Trooper Stephen Hall, was northbound on U.S. Highway 285 near FairPlay, in Park County Colorado. I overheard Pueblo Regional Communication Center (PRCC) report a two-vehicle crash on U.S. Highway 285 near Mile Point 208 in Park County. I informed PRCC that I would respond to the crash, but my arrival may be extended due to snow and icy roads. I arrived on scene at approximately 2055 hours.

Upon arrival, I observed an SUV in the southbound lane facing west and a white single axle box truck in a creek off the northbound shoulder. The SUV had severe damage to the driver's side. There were several fire and EMS personnel standing around the driver's door of the SUV where the driver appeared to be trapped. I asked the driver, a younger adult white male with a bald head, what happened and he replied he did not remember. The driver then asked about the passenger, his girlfriend. The EMS personnel informed the driver that his girlfriend was in an ambulance and being transported to Denver. The driver was visibly shaking and cold so he was provided a blanket.

After checking on the SUV driver I started asking some of the onlookers nearby if they had observed the crash. No one reported seeing the crash occur, however, one individual did report he administered CPR to the passenger of the SUV prior to the arrival of EMS personnel. I requested he complete a witness statement due to his involvement and he agreed. I then requested him and any other person not involved in extricating the driver to return to their vehicles. Everyone complied with my instructions except for two younger Hispanic males who had been driving the box truck. They were uninjured but were unable to return to their vehicle due to its location in the vegetation off of the northbound shoulder.

I asked the driver of the box truck what happened. He told me they were northbound when they saw the SUV sliding sideways toward them in their lane. The driver said he attempted to apply the brakes and avoid the vehicle but his actions were ineffective due to the icy road and falling snow. I requested the driver of the box truck to complete a driver's statement and he complied with my request. I instructed the two men to get in one of the fire trucks for their safety while they completed the driver's statement.

At this point, I attempted to get a status on the passenger of the SUV and was informed by an EMS technician that her condition was deteriorating and *they were going to transport her immediately. I thanked him for the information and then returned to my patrol car. At my patrol car, I updated PRCC and other responding Troopers of the passenger's condition and my observations. I then moved my patrol car to better facilitate traffic control while the driver was extricated from the SUV.*

****

That's all I have, as far as memory goes, to inform me of the moment that changed my life. For such a huge and monumental moment, one that has caused a colossal amount of pain, hurt, and hardship in my life...a police report is all that I have to try and explain to me what the *hell* happened that night. This is my story of what happened to completely flip my life upside down and how I've reoriented myself to try and figure out this new life I was given. The good, the bad, the painful and the most rewarding experiences I've had in my thirty-three years of living. This is my side of the story. Don't get me wrong, I'm aware this accident had a huge impact on many people's lives, but this is how it has changed my life. I don't share this story in hopes to get sympathy from anyone, or to trivialize or compare traumas; I don't see your situation and raise it with my brain injury. My trauma doesn't make your situation any less of a trauma. I write this with the best-case, idealistic outcome in mind: that you can find a relatable experience and find inspiration and hope if you ever find yourself in a hopeless circumstance. I want you to see that no matter what is thrown your way, there's always a way forward...it just may look a little different than what you expected.

The morning of, I appreciated the subtle breeze that cooled down the blaring sun that beat down on me as I took my dog for a walk. Colorado has never ceased to amaze me with its unpredictable weather; in this case it was unusually warm for a January day. I have proof of the warmth because I sent a Snapchat of me taking my dog on a walk with the temperature displayed across the screen. It was the nice weather that inspired a mountain getaway for my boyfriend, Jeremy, and I. We decided to drive to his mountain house and stay the night so we could avoid the grid-locked traffic that we, along with the rest of Colorado, usually had to endure on Saturday mornings. During our drive up the mountain a storm rolled in but being a native of Colorado and both of us being used to Colorado's arbitrary weather, we didn't worry. We just figured it was going to add more time to our trip. We continued on our familiar route to get to our mountain-house destination. The pass isn't one of the aggressive mountain passes with the hairpin turns. It's a two-lane road that gently bends as it guides drivers and provides a way to traverse the mountainous terrain. It's a common spot that attracts locals and visitors for the views. As we drove the familiar route that often moonlighted as our weekend getaway, we let the stunning sights pass us by as unappreciated luxuries that we had become all too used to. In the northbound lane, traveling towards us, a box-truck was returning from a delivery that had turned out to be a three-hour task instead of the quick twenty-minute drop-off like planned. We learned his longer-than-anticipated drop-off was because he got stuck in a ditch while he was backing out of a driveway. Once the driver finally freed himself, he started his trek back to Denver so he could clock out and go home. He didn't bother to put the chains on the tires despite the law put in place, due to the storm; and even given his most recent encounter with the ditch, he still didn't bother to follow the rules. I'll never know why he neglected to obey the law and put chains on his tires, but I can assume it was a "not-so-heavy-choice," and one made in an attempt to end his shift sooner. I like to think there's no way he would choose to forego the chains knowing the foreboding fate that lay in his future. Regardless, his tires slipped on the icy roads, causing a hectic pursuit of safety and maddening swerving in attempts to miss him. Ultimately, we found ourselves in a car with a semi-truck barreling directly towards us leaving us two decisions: one—react and dodge him further but tumble to our death off the mountain or two—collide into him. We did the latter of the two.

I was the worst hurt in the accident and suffered a traumatic brain injury. An atlanto-occipital dislocation (AOD) or in layman's terms, an internal decapitation. Basically, the vertebra that connects the skull to the spinal cord was snapped but it didn't cause damage to the spinal cord which is why I still have use of my limbs and I, thankfully, avoided paralysis. This type of injury has a mortality rate of seventy percent, and of the remaining thirty percent that live, half of those survivors die in the ambulance on the way to the hospital. That's an EIGHTY FIVE PERCENT FATALITY RATE…and that's just one of my injuries. I spent months after the accident in a coma. My twenty-ninth birthday was one of those days. While I lay lifeless in a hospital room, hooked up to machines keeping me alive, my friends and family gathered in the waiting room telling each other stories that involved me.

Remembering the joyous times spent with the lifeless patient who now occupied room 19 in the Neuro ICU of St. Anthony's Hospital in Lakewood, CO.

I'm sure my family was there sharing stories of how I was the "bossy-pants" of the family in a lovingly manner and joking kind of way. I hope my younger sister could remember me encouraging her to go after her dreams in activism work by going back to school and obtaining her college degree. Hopefully my younger brother reminisced about the many laughs we shared; being so close in age we often joked we were twins. My youngest sister probably laughed thinking about the times we would go out to Target and pretend she was my daughter rather than sister. She's sixteen years younger than me so we would pretend I was the teen mom, all the while talking in fake British accents. (Don't ask me why we did these things, but we thought we were hilarious.) My older sister…well, she probably wasn't there seeing as how we hadn't seen her in years. In fairness, how would she know her sister was involved in a terrible accident and was left desperately clinging onto life? She was probably worrying about where and how she was going to get her next high. Her addiction first started as a cocaine addiction but, after being prescribed pills for a back surgery and with the easy access to opioids, it left her with an addiction to pills. The addiction has turned into a full-fledged heroin, meth, opioid, and any-other-drug-that's-out-there addiction. It has taken over her life and placed drugs as a number one priority; above friends, above family, above her own daughters…above herself, really. We've struggled with trying to get her help, and with a short-lived stint of sobriety, she now has no desire to get clean. If I can share only one thing through this sixteen-plus year battle with drugs, it's this: you can't force someone into sobriety. They must be willing to try, and ultimately, they have to want it.

My mom and I are no strangers to hospital waiting rooms but usually she's the patient. I was by her side in every chemotherapy treatment she had and all five surgeries when she was going through her diagnosis of breast cancer. (That doesn't even account for her thirty-five rounds of radiation she went through.) Now, she was by my side when I needed her most. I'm sure my dad was there, too, providing his comfort in his presence rather than words. He's a very quiet guy but it's not to be confused with a lack of concern or care. He just thinks in his own head a lot. We have a bond that only he and I can explain.

My friends were there, too. I grew up with a group of nine or ten girlfriends that were more like sisters than friends. I always thought our friendship was an exception to most girlfriend groups...we were special. It started with a few of us as friends. Well, really, if I'm explaining it from my point of view, it started in third grade when two girls, Ella and Kasey, befriended me. We became thick as thieves. They were my two, very best of friends going forward through middle school, high school, and even through college. All throughout elementary school we spent every recess together and had many after-school snacks together. We were at each other's house's so often we took back ways and knew the best shortcuts. As each year went by, we graduated from each grade and entered the next surrounded by the same kids in our class, essentially keeping the same group of twenty-seven kids together. From grades three to six I was with the same kids, just a different teacher each year. Seventh grade was the big change. Not only was it a different building, but it was when we went to different classrooms for each subject. I was no longer going to be taught social studies, English, math, and science with the same group of twenty-seven kids. Here, our world was about to broaden. I was going to have classes with other kids in different classrooms; kids from different schools previously; kids who lived in different towns from me. This middle school had three different "teams" the kids were split up in: A, B, or C. "A" team had one set of teachers, "B" team had another set, and "C" team had their own set of teachers. What that meant was you shared classes with other students on your team. Ella, Kasey, and I were all assigned different teams, which meant we all had different classes. We shared the same middle school but that's about it. Once we got to the school, the seven hours spent inside were spent completely different and on our own. I made my own friends with girls that were in my classes on team A, Kasey made friends with girls in her classes on team B, and Ella made friends with girls in her classes on team C. However Ella, Kasey, and I remained friends and soon our sleepovers consisted of more than just us three—they included the other friends we each met from our teams. Soon passing periods became five-minute breaks to see our friends on different teams. My group of three (me, Ella, and Kasey) became a group of ten-plus girls. Heidi, Mallory, Delia, Moira, Jessa, Morgan, Cara, Mel, Beth, and Brooke. We spent every weekend together. We played sports together. We knew which boy each girl liked. With how much time we spent together, my parents gained nine new daughters, and likewise, their families gained another daughter in me. Starting in seventh grade, these girls became an integral part of my life. We graduated middle school together and found our ways through high school together. We experienced first boyfriends and first dates, awkward school dances, school basketball, and volleyball games. We shared excitement as each one of us turned sixteen and got our driver's license. Getting a driver's license led to breaking curfew with each other and drinking in the basement together. We never got into drugs, though. That's one thing I'm still so thankful we were all smart enough not to try and even be tempted by. We were a good group of girls. I remember early on, probably in seventh grade, we all had a big sleep-over (at Moira's house, I remember) and we all addressed the nonsense drama we were dealing with. Ya know, rumors. "Brooke said this about Cara..." or "Did you see Delia's hair??? How stupid does that look?" Stupid things all girls go through. We all decided we were not going to partake in that kind of drama and it wasn't necessary nor acceptable. I look back at it and am so impressed by how mature all of us handled it. Here we were, a group of thirteen-year-old girls, and we all decided we're not going to talk badly about each other to someone else, and if there is anything that needs to be addressed we would bring it up to that person directly. Our honesty with each other would squash any unwanted and unnecessary drama. From that moment on, we were best of friends. We would continue to be best friends through middle school and high school, with the occasional girl moving away, but for the most part, our main group of eight or nine stayed the same. We all went to different colleges; a few of us stayed in state and most went out of state.

I started at one in-state school, the University of Colorado at Boulder (CU Buffs), and transferred to another in-state university not too long after, Colorado State University (CSU Rams). I would tell most people it's because CSU had a more specific program for my major, which is true. But if I'm being completely honest, it's because I was so unhappy at CU. I didn't have my group of girlfriends I grew up with. I had acquaintances—people I knew because we went to the same high school, but we weren't as close. At the time, I saw it more like I went off to college alone. Even though it was only a forty-minute drive from home, I ended up leaving the college town *Every. Single. Weekend.* I still had my job in my hometown so I could use that as an excuse, but really, I didn't want to spend the weekends at college. I had a much harder time making friendships that were as strong as the ones I had in high school. But my main best friend, the one who I've always had a special bond with—Kasey, she went to Colorado State University which was only about an hour away from my school. On the rare weekends that I wouldn't go home, I would go up to visit her. Kasey had made a group of close friends. (Kasey's much more outgoing than I am. She's also very funny and fun to be around. She's more like the "life-of-the-party" type of girl whereas I'm not. I'm always the friend of the "life-of-the-party"…the "plus one" that's always around.) I didn't even make it one full semester at Boulder until I realized Boulder was not the life for me. I started looking into transferring to CSU so by the second semester I could start at CSU. The major I wanted at CSU required you to apply for it because it was only open for three hundred students per year. It was a competitive major and not one for slackers. But it didn't matter, I wanted a pre-med major. Colorado State offered a Biomedical Science major which had more of a direction than the general Biology major offered at CU. Not only was I accepted into CSU but I got accepted into the biomedical science program, so at the beginning of my second semester I moved up to Fort Collins to attend Colorado State University and left Boulder as a part of my past. I was now a ram and not a buff. (Go Rammies!) When I moved up to Fort Collins, Kasey made my transition so much easier. She introduced me to her friends she had already made, so any time not spent studying, I had acquaintances to fill my time and any void. Kasey even got me an on-campus job as a receptionist at the IT department she worked at. I had friends to spend my lunchtime with or eat dinner with. I started to get my routine up there; Kasey and I would go to the gym to work out at night, we knew her dorm had the better breakfast food but mine had the better selection for dinners. She and I would find time in the middle of our class schedules to meet up and share lunch at our favorite soup and salad spot on campus. My life was transitioning from the lonely one to a more social one that involved friends. College went on for the next four years, with Kasey and I living together until we graduated. When we graduated, we got a place in Denver with two of our friends from the original high school group. They moved back from their out of state colleges and we all just picked up where we left off. Life was great. We all had different jobs and were professional twenty-three-year-olds during the week, but on weekends we could hit the town and drink and dance the night away. Life was good. Life was normal. I was living the life that you would expect a normal twenty-something would be living. I had a job, a solid group of friends, a healthy family life, and a dog.

One thing that I've always struggled with is my personal life, meaning my personal "boyfriend" life. I've never had trouble getting along with the opposite sex, but often I found myself in the best friend zone. I think it had something to do with my looks…I had really bad acne growing up. So bad it was socially debilitating. The kind that looks painful. I remember there would be times I'd be at a friend's house and the parents would ask me, "Oh no! what happened!?" and I'd have to tell the embarrassing fact that it was just a zit. That was never asked with malicious intent. The zit often popped, forming an open wound on my face so they didn't look like the typical zit, it looked like something happened to give me this cut on my face…which led to the question. Nonetheless, it happened numerous times. Another struggle that really helped drive home my self-confidence issues were sleepovers I had with friends growing up. The thought of friends seeing me without makeup was terrifying. I knew which foundations would last me through the night, so long as I slept with my head facing the ceiling all night to keep the makeup from rubbing off onto the pillow. Either way, I always made sure I would wake up before the group so I could sneak a morning reapplication of makeup in the bathroom.

You would think I'd be good at makeup from all of my experience with it, but sadly you'd be mistaken to think that. I look back at pictures and my face color is always different. It looks like I'm a ghost or a Japanese Geisha with my face always being a startling white or I'm an awkward shade of orange resembling Donald Trump.

Matching my foundation to my skin color was always a struggle and not to mention I always left my mark wherever I went…literally. If I touched my face, my fingers would get some of the foundation on them so anything I touched after left an orange-ish fingerprint.

As gruesome as it is for me to explain my embarrassing past, everyone around me was kind enough to just pretend they didn't see the acne. Everyone—teachers, friends, parents of friends, friends of friends. It was a sort of "don't-ask-don't-tell" situation. I remember one time a group of us were all playing at a park on a weekend, outside of school, and we decided to play spin the bottle. When one of the boy's turn came around, he spun it and it landed on me and he was hesitant. He didn't want to play. The rest of the kids were giving him a hard time and heckling him saying, "C'mon, you gotta do it! Those are the rules…" but he was really hesitant and even stormed away from the circle. When one of his buddies went to go after him and bring him back to the circle, I overheard him say, "Whatever man, I'm not gonna kiss her! I'm not gonna put my mouth anywhere near that…I don't want to get whatever she has," (insinuating my acne was contagious). What makes me cringe even more thinking back on it, is after he said it, one of the guys was like, "C'mon man, don't say that…that's harsh," and even the girls sort of gathered around me to comfort me. Which is so unbelievably nice, but also embarrassing to think of how much everyone was pitying me.

To say the least, I had a hard time growing up with my image complex. I couldn't control my skin; it didn't matter the prescription products I tried or the number of times I washed my face. The breakouts still happened and they happened relentlessly. With that said, it's easy to see how I never had a boyfriend. I mean, I had a boyfriend in like fourth grade, but we were such little kids I think it was more because we were the two black kids in class (I'm part black) so everyone thought, "OK, you two are together." Either way, once we broadened our social circles and met other people going to middle school and high school, I never had dates to dances or a boyfriend to meet up with during passing periods…but I had my girls. I didn't need a boy to make me happy.

As I grew up my acne calmed down. I no longer suffered from the angry backlash of breakouts but my skin was far from perfect. I still had the lasting issues about my complexion that lingered from my childhood. For example, being seen in public with no makeup wasn't an option. It just *never* happened. But as the years went by it didn't hold such a strong grip on me and no longer debilitated me to live my life. I started dating boys even though the words "boyfriend/girlfriend" were never used. In all of my relationships we never got to that point. I never found myself in a serious enough relationship to call him my boyfriend…and that was his choice. Well, at least I assumed it was his choice. I never had that kind of talk with anyone before because I didn't want to be that needy girl. I wanted to be the cool, chill girl whose boyfriend's buddies looked at with jealousy. I wanted them to look at me and my "boyfriend" and think, *Man, he's so lucky he got a good girl.* The relationship wasn't serious enough for me to be considered their girlfriend so they certainly weren't serious enough to meet any of my family members. Being in a different city 1.5 hours north of my family made it easy to separate those two worlds. The first "boyfriend" I brought home (I put quotes around that word because we never established the boyfriend/girlfriend status) was after I graduated college. And it wasn't even like a dinner or some kind of occasion introducing him to my parents. He helped me move back into my parents' house after college. I don't even think my dad was home…maybe he was, he literally dropped off my dresser and TV and then we drove back to Fort Collins to go out that night.

Fast-forward to the years I lived with my girlfriends right out of college, and I still didn't have a boyfriend. I had a constant or regular guy to call and we would hook up but looking back on it, it was really nothing more than a late-night hook-up/booty call. He never met my parents, I never met his, I never even met his friends…we were never seen out in daylight hours together. I'd usually send/receive a text at midnight and we'd meet up at his house around 1:00 or 2:00 a.m. I NEVER stayed the night because he lived at his parents'…when he did get his own place I still never stayed the night…I don't know why; it was just something we never did.

I dated other guys and had my flings, but again, no talk of "boyfriend" with any of the guys. It wasn't until I was twenty-seven that a friend invited a guy she knew to my house. She had told me her twin sister had introduced them originally with the idea of those two getting together. After a date my friend knew nothing was going to come of the two of them but she told me, "Mol, I think you guys would be good together. You should meet him!" He was an MMA fighter and just returning back from a fight he had in Canada. His friends were hosting a welcome home party for him and my friend tried to get me to go along with her. I declined because I thought that would look too groupie-like on my part, so she invited him to my house one night we were all casually drinking. That's the night our love story began but I'll share more of our love story later. More to come…I first want to finish on letting you know who I am. I've primarily focused on letting you know who I used to be, before the accident, but I realize I haven't said a word on who I am after the accident.

My brain injury has left me severely disabled and unable to work (to date…I told the doctors to be prepared for me to prove them wrong about their prognosis that I'll never work again). Since I was fifteen and got a worker's permit, I've always had a job, so being unemployed was a drastic and uncomfortable fact I had to cope with. I had to find ways to fill the hours that made my days. I used to schedule my days around TV shows. I could turn the early morning news on at 6:30, then watch *The Today Show* through the nine o'clock hour. I didn't care for the local programming that was on at 10:00 so I'd turn the TV off and do my therapies until 3:00 rolled around, when *The Ellen DeGeneres Show* came on. (I watched that religiously—I would schedule my therapies around it.) By the time Ellen ended at 4:00, it was close enough to the evening news and dinner that I could easily find ways to pass time until 8:00. Then at 8:00…it was bedtime. I know that sounds early, but that's a full fourteen hours from my waking hour…that's a lot of empty hours to fill. I didn't even have to be tired or sleepy to be excited for bedtime, I just successfully filled fourteen hours—sleep was my reward.

At first what I thought to myself was *Is THIS what my days have turned into? What am I supposed to do?* The shock of my days opening up became a huge change for me. From walking twenty blocks to work, daily, to nothing. I couldn't even walk from my room at the back of my house to the centrally located family room. I felt stir-crazy; like I was supposed to be doing something, but I had nothing to be done. Never for second did I accept that this is what my life was going to look like.

Once I moved out of my parents' and into Jeremy's townhouse, he must've noticed my wasted potential, so he asked if I would like to accompany him in volunteering. At the time, he volunteered for Reading Partners, "a national nonprofit that mobilizes communities to provide students with the proven, individualized reading support they need to read at grade level by fourth grade." He went to the elementary school that was less than a mile away, every Wednesday, to work with his student to get them to reading level. At first, I would just go with him and sit in on his sessions offering a second way to get the reading strategy but, by all means, Jeremy was the tutor. I was just there shadowing him. A few weeks into the tutoring, Jeremy asked me if I'd like to lead the lesson. I was hesitant because my speech was noticeably affected by the TBI but it was still understandable—I thought it was worse than what it actually was…I'm judgmental of it just like everyone is upon hearing their own voice played back to them on a recorder. I voiced my concerns and hesitations with Jeremy to which he reassured me it would be fine and he reminded me that in the worst-case scenario, he'll be right there with me and can step in to help. Jeremy was the nudge I needed to push through my insecurities. I finished the year out taking a bigger role in Jeremy's sessions than just a shadow. I felt more confident in offering help to ensure this student had adequate reading skills. The following year I upped my game and got my own student to tutor; Jeremy would drive us to the school in the morning, we would tutor our own individual students in the one forty-five-minute session, then Jeremy would drop me off at our townhome before he drove off to work. Once I got a scooter I was able to use it as a way to transport me to and from the school on my own. I no longer depended on Jeremy for a ride so I could increase my volunteer hours. I went from one session once a week to four sessions a day, four days a week.

I gained just as much, if not more, from tutoring than the students gained from me. Tutoring gave me back a sense of purpose. The highlight of my day went from being the hour spent watching *The Ellen DeGeneres Show* to seeing the lightbulb go off in a child's mind when teaching the long sound of a vowel. Or maybe we had a tough session and the curriculum was harder to grasp, but I had a learning moment come up that taught a life lesson—like being kind or the importance of using manners. These kids quickly gained a space in my heart; I got to know them and their individual quirks just like they came to know me and my quirks. I remember when I was learning to walk; I used a cane to help me with my balance in situations that required longer distances. When I first started walking I had my cane with me at all times but as I progressed I wanted to make sure I didn't depend on it. I didn't want it to become an unnecessary crutch like a baby's blanket. I figured tutoring was an appropriate place for me to walk without a cane. Once I got in the building, I'd park my scooter in the front office and walk down the hall to the room where tutoring took place. There really wasn't much walking involved so a cane wasn't necessary. I had a plan in my head to go to tutoring without my cane. This was a big deal...to me. The morning I left the townhouse I had to give myself a pep talk to reassure myself I could do this. Once I got to the school and I picked up my first student for her session she looked at me and asked me with excited curiosity in her voice, "Miss Molei, where's your walky-stick thing?" When I told her I wasn't using it that day she said, "Because your walking's getting so good?" I smiled back and could cry tears of joy and gratitude for her noticing my small accomplishment.

The local news has done a few stories on my accident and they did one on my involvement in the school. Since it was filmed in the elementary school and a few of the students were interviewed, the school showed it in a morning assembly and invited me to be a "guest of honor." After seeing the news story, the kids viewed me as being famous and it was as if a celebrity was roaming the halls. It was adorable and humbling seeing the kids act that way but I also used the "fame" to my advantage. With the kids that had shorter attention spans, or it was just harder to get them engaged in schoolwork, I would say that I only tutored the kids who were smart enough to be with me. I would frame it as an honor to be paired with me; that I only tutored the best behaved and smartest kids. I would tell the students they had to prove to the coordinator that they could be my student. I thought I was tricking the kids into learning and I thought they only wanted to be my student because I was "famous," but these kids genuinely cared for me. One time I was walking a kid down the hall when another student was walking the other way towards us. When we crossed paths, the other student said to me,

"You walk like a retard…you should learn how to walk!" As quickly as it took me to realize this kid was bullying me, my student stepped in front of the bully and yelled, "DON'T SPEAK TO HER LIKE THAT! NO ONE TALKS TO MISS MOLEI LIKE THAT!" I had to quickly intervene and tell the boys not to fight while gently guiding them separate ways. My student went on, saying, "But Miss, he was making fun of you!" I told him I heard him making fun of me but I didn't care because I can't let comments like that bother me. My heart grew two sizes that day.

Before the accident I didn't know how much I could care about education; to be more specific, the fundamental, beginning reading skills. Volunteering with Reading Partners has become a huge part of my life and it has given me a new passion in life. It's given me a new cause to fight for: I want every kid to have the opportunity to succeed in their future. Reading is at the very base of that opportunity and one that other opportunities arise from. In retrospect, taking an overall look at all of this, one connection I can make (and I didn't even notice it until a friend kindly pointed it out to me), is that this accident has shown me how to slow down and respect the basics. It's easy to get caught up in the hustle and bustle of things and get so tunnel-visioned when your eyes are focused on the finish line, and the finish line ONLY. But we overlook the present and how much there is to be grateful for. It's important to focus and take time on the basics, like me relearning to swallow or the kids learning to read, because it's those basics that you can build upon to make greatness. As long as you always try, never give up, and have good intentions in every single thing you do, you can do great things to help improve this world. Just have patience, keep your head down, work hard, and enjoy your time as it is…not for what you hope it'll be but for what it is RIGHT. NOW.

CHAPTER THREE-
JEREMY

I didn't fall in love with Jeremy at the hospital; if anything, the hospital just reaffirmed our love. Of course people can fall in love with each other in luxurious, romantic sceneries (I'm thinking of *The Bachelor/Bachelorette* dates where they spend their time on a private sailboat in the Cayman Islands or being serenaded by a famous musician in their own personal concert). This kind of scenery makes it easier to confuse the romantic scene set up by producers for true, *genuine,* romantic feelings of love.

Jeremy and I didn't have that. Our love story consisted of ambulance rides instead of hot air balloons and the incessant beeping of the breathing monitors rather than the romantic tune of a love song. I'm not sure if I can pinpoint a specific time or event as when I knew I was in love, but looking back at his devotion and dedication to me while I was in a coma makes me more confident that he loves me just as much as I love him. Jeremy's always there for me.

Him being a part of my life has been the most positive thing that has ever happened to me. When he first came into my life, it wasn't like I dreamed about the possibility of us. I didn't imagine introducing him to my friends as my boyfriend…there were no moments of me scribbling "Molei Osheim" on my notepad. Not to say I wasn't interested in him. The night we met, we had a good conversation about snowboarding/skiing. (At least he tells me it was good. I got too drunk and don't remember our conversation.) The idea of us as a couple was more like a fleeting thought dancing by; it was fun and nice to think about, but I didn't spend enough time thinking about it to yearn for it. It was a year before the two of us would finally go on a date, and during that time if any thoughts did pop in my mind about Jeremy, I never gave them life by sharing them with friends. I think that was my way of protecting myself; that way, if nothing came of it, I couldn't be disappointed nor let down. No one knew about him; therefore, I couldn't be disappointed. I couldn't fail.

There were many loosely scheduled snowboarding/skiing trips that never came to fruition. Many "I'm headed up to the mountains, I can give you a ride if you want…" Then I would text some excuse the morning of, explaining why I couldn't make it. Our plans downgraded from riding up together, to meeting once we each got to the mountain. Even then, we never met up. Then it went from the hopes of meeting up on the weekends to being Snapchat acquaintances. We didn't even have a friendship worthy enough of texting. Becoming Snapchat friends allowed us to keep enough distance and not talk, but send a quick picture of the fun party we were at or the luxurious scenery we were taking in to remind each other of our existence. A sort of insurance, to make sure we didn't fall off the face of the Earth and to keep us relevant.

Either way, we stayed relevant enough to finally get a

date on the books and stick to it. I remember, in the car ride home from the restaurant, my feelings hit me fast. Up to that point in the night everything had been so easy. So much so, it didn't even occur to me that we were on a date. There were no brief moments of panic trying to think of something to say to fill the awkward silence. I was able to speak to him about anything. I talked about my family, my friends, my hobbies, my work, my hopes, and my passions...I wouldn't be surprised if I talked about world problems and some ambitious resolution. The night was going so seamlessly I forgot I was on a date. All the pressures of the first date were nowhere to be found... until the car ride home. I remember thinking, *I'm soooo surprised at how easy and nice this night has been. It's not like any other first date I've been on....CRAP...I'M ON A DATE! That means there might be a goodnight kiss.* I found myself frantically predicting situations of how it would go in my head. I thought of using the front door instead of the garage because that would be more of a natural walk for him rather than stumbling and climbing over all my junk in the garage. Then I planned on just being natural: *If he goes in for a kiss, let it happen. If it's a hug, that's fine too!* I thought to myself, *Just be natural, Mol!!!*

HA! None of that happened. I guess I got out of the car, ABRUPTLY, when we got home. Jeremy says I practically jumped out while it was still in motion. I remember it a little differently. I remember he pulled up to my driveway and I sheepishly fiddled with the door handle and acted like I couldn't find it in the dark which would allow him a reason to lean in closer to me and go for a kiss. But the kiss never came and I could only fumble with the handle so long before I was forced to make my exit.

After that first date, I found myself thinking about him. He was the first person I wanted to share my good news with. If I saw something funny, I wanted to share a laugh with him. Soon I was noticing small things that reminded me of Jeremy. The brand of whiskey at a restaurant was the same kind of whiskey Jeremy had on our date…every time I saw a VW Passat I thought of him because that was the type of car he had. Our relationship progressed from a Snapchat acquaintance to texting throughout the day. We went on more dates and soon my weekends were filled with time spent with him. Soon, I would regularly spend the night at his apartment. His roommates quickly became used to seeing me around. I no longer knocked on the door; rather I would just walk into the apartment and say hi to his roommates watching TV in the living room as I went upstairs to his room. Jeremy's friendship came easily to me. I never had to fake how I felt. If I was upset because I watched a documentary on climate change or on starving kids in Africa, Jeremy was there not only to listen, but he would engage in conversation with me. We would go snowboarding/skiing together in the winter. Then when the sun transformed the snowcapped mountains to daffodil-filled trails, we would go hiking together. He taught me how to play golf and he played on my grass volleyball team when we needed a sub. Soon, those documentaries were enjoyed by watching them together.

Each day we spent together, I learned more and more little things about him. For example, I knew he had a passion for public service. At the time, he worked for Denver Public Schools—he was in the communication department, but, nonetheless, his first and foremost priority was improving children's education. He also volunteered, teaching elementary school students how to read. I knew he shared my concerns with the environment and we both cared about climate change. He knew my broad taste in music so I could appreciate any song he shared with me. We had "date nights" where we would volunteer together at the local shelter making meals to serve to homeless people. I could be all the Molei's with him: The passionate one who thought of things I could do, personally, to help with climate change. The competitive one playing setter on my volleyball team. The goofy one who could laugh at myself when I danced to the most recent Beyoncé or Lady Gaga song. The geeky one when I got in a deep conversation about the devastation deforestation has on us after watching a documentary about it. Or the lazy one when I just wanted to turn my brain off and laugh while I watched an episode of *Friends*. The more we became an "us," the thing I really appreciated was the boundaries we kept, ensuring we both didn't lose our individual "I's." I still had my life and he still had his. I still felt comfortable going to weekend trips away with my friends without him. I wanted the best for him and he wanted the best for me. I was able to share goals with him and he would push me to reach them. More importantly, he would celebrate my successes.

I can't remember any huge blow-up fights I had with him before the accident. Once, we were driving and another car cut us off so badly it ran us out of our lane, so we were forced to exit the highway. Since our cars were both now using the same exit, there was a stoplight that we were both stopped at, and the two of them, the two drivers, started yelling back and forth between the rolled-down windows. It got so heated that the other driver got out of his car to seem all big and bad, so Jeremy got out of his. Now Jeremy's a big guy; a muscular guy standing at 6'6", so as soon as Jeremy got out of the car the other, littler guy was stunned, looking like a deer caught in headlights with eyes as big as silver dollars. He turned around to go sit back in his car and waited for the light to turn green. Once the other guy turned around sheepishly, Jeremy didn't keep going; he got back in his car, but I was still ravaged with anger and embarrassment. Jeremy knew I was not happy, too. I didn't even like it when he yelled at the driver or flipped them the bird, let alone got out of the car. That's the only time I can remember being upset with Jeremy and even in that, we talked about why I was so upset and we talked it through. Like two adults. I found myself in a relationship that was fun, intellectually stimulating, and motivating, and even when I found myself upset or frustrated, we were able to be reasonable about it. I seemed to have found myself a perfect partner.

Jeremy's and my relationship went through a drastic, life-altering event so early on in its existence, that it is remarkable where we are today. We had only been officially exclusive for two short months before the accident happened. I went from a girl in a new relationship with simple worries such as not letting him see me without makeup on or with my hair curly, to the hurt girl who had much bigger worries like needing help going to the bathroom or showering. Early on in the hospital, I couldn't even sit up on my own, so I certainly didn't have the luxury of worrying about straightening my hair. When I was an inpatient at Craig, the nurses would shower me every two days. What used to be considered a normal task quickly turned into a scheduled ordeal because I couldn't sit myself up. This involved a big swing contraption that was on tracks on the ceiling. The nurses would position me in the straps so then they could press a button that would lift me from my supine position in bed, to a seated position, to my wheelchair. Then they could wheel me to my bathroom and help transfer me to a commode, a chair-like device with a hole in the seat that would allow you to place a trash can under and use it like a toilet. All the normal, everyday tasks now turned into bigger challenges to overcome. I wasn't able to do anything that comes automatically; walking, sitting up, breathing. I couldn't talk and I couldn't eat, I couldn't even go to the bathroom— I had a catheter for that. Once I was well enough to get that removed, I still needed help getting to the bathroom, which was just one of the simple, basic, everyday tasks I required help in doing.

Trauma has a huge part in our love story. I see it in two ways: one—so romantic. I have the love story only seen in movies. Girl gets in coma and boy stays by her side because the love is too strong to leave. Or two—tragic. I can also see it as a tragic love story. Our relationship only had the two months to experience the simple pleasures every other couple gets to experience. Things like conversation through a meal. Or going to concerts together, or on hikes with one another, or skiing together, or the simple night out on the town together. My love story doesn't have your typical firsts that are found in every other story, like the first time living with a boy or the first time you say, "I love you." The accident robbed me of all the cute firsts.

The first time I lived with a boyfriend involved us living at my parents' house post-accident. The first time I heard "I love you" from a boy other than my dad or brother was when I was in Craig Hospital. I had a chest x-ray scheduled, so someone from radiology would come to my room to wheel my bed off to the x-ray room. When she came in, she asked me, "Are you ready to get your x-ray? It won't take us long," to which I smiled to show my obligatory participation. Jeremy was in the room with me and as the x-ray tech pushed my bed out of the room, he said, "K babe, I'll be right here when you get back. I love you." My eyes immediately widened and I thought to myself, *Are we doing that now?!? We've never said that to each other before*! Remember, I still couldn't speak, so I couldn't yell back, "I LOVE YOU TOO!"; my neck is fused so I can't even turn my head to look back at him and give some sort of eye contact. In internal shock to what he had just said, I had to lie in my bed motionless, as it was being pushed down the hall. On the way to get my chest x-ray, anyone who saw me being pushed down the halls saw the happiest bedridden patient with the biggest grin on her face. I must've been a perfect picture for the word oxymoron: a bedridden hospital patient who couldn't be happier or have a bigger smile on her face.

Though the accident robbed me of all the cute firsts, it's a slippery slope to see it this way. I have to intentionally avoid thinking about all the things this accident has taken from me or else it's too easy to fall into a dark hole and be suffocated by depressing thoughts. Jeremy and I have been through more than any other couple should ever have to go through, but it's because of all we've gone through that we are so strong. Thinking of the silver lining prevents me from looking at our story in a negative way.

When I woke up from the coma, I immediately felt a

sense of gratitude for him. I had a yearning for him that came so effortlessly to me. It's like it was natural, like it was built into my DNA. Jeremy had become an essential part of my life. After I came out of my comatose state, I still couldn't talk and I had little control over some of the involuntary movements. One, in particular, was uncontrollably sitting up and down. I went from being the girl from *The Exorcist*—constantly sitting up for no reason at all- to the mute girl stuck in her own body.

Very soon doctors were able to use a thing for yes/no questions. Essentially, it was an orange cut-out frame with the word "yes" on the top part and "no" on the bottom. They would hold the box so it framed their face and ask me yes/no questions, then track my eyes. If I looked up it meant "yes," down meant "no." Shortly after, they were able to use eye movement as a tracker, and they were able to teach me how to use a machine that served as a robotic voice for me. I could use it, with my gaze, to communicate with the outside world. The first time in speech therapy, my speech therapist (ST) taught me how to use it. There were certain messages I could stare at and if my eyes held gaze long enough over a phrase, that's the one it chose. For example, one phrase would be "I feel…", then if I held gaze at it for two seconds it would automatically bring me to a screen that gave me option like "cold," "sick," "tired," etc. I could form basic sentences like these; not the most captivating conversation topics, but enough to get me the basics. One of the screens gave me an option of a phrase "I want…," so I stared at that and it brought me to the next screen of options like "water," "food," "sleep," but it also had a keyboard option where I could stare at a letter and it would let me spell out a word. I knew I needed to do that. My speech therapist grabbed her pen and was held captivated by the machine. "Yes Molei...tell us what you want. We're here for you..." I started spelling the word out with my eyes. My eyes went straight to the "J." A robotic voice said aloud, "J." On to the next letter: E...and on to the next. I continued this with the letters R-E-M-Y. "Jeremy! You want Jeremy," my speech therapist read back to me. It was the first time I could communicate to the outside world what I wanted. She assured me that he would be back tonight, but he still needed to work and it was the middle of the day. I was quickly reminded of the fact that the world didn't stop just because mine did. The sun still rose and set, tides still came in and went out, the tedium of daily life continued, only mine was stopped in mid-track and I was shoved back to start. My tasks now consisted of learning how to breathe on my own and how to talk/communicate. Once I got the very basics down, learning while I was inpatient, I could bump up to harder tasks, like eating solids, or drinking liquids, which would take place during outpatient care. Walking wasn't even talked about while I was at Craig as an inpatient. The "harder tasks" I'm referring to is all stuff I could do based on my recovery once I got discharged. I was discharged with a feeding tube still in place; eating and drinking came later. Basically, the hospital wanted to make sure I could survive going home. THEN once I could accomplish the bare minimum, I could work on all the extras, like eating and drinking. Then, eventually, walking would come if I was willing to do the hard work and therapy.

I like to think Jeremy had a similar need for me—it wasn't even a question that he needed to spend time at the hospital with me. It was probably a conscious decision made on his part to stay with me; but, in any case, he spent every night with me. He slept with me in my hospital bed enduring hourly check-ins by nurses and vital checks. He would wake up early to accommodate for the commute to work and still, every day after work, instead of going home to unwind from the nightmare his life had abruptly become, he came back to the hospital to spend the time with me. Our time together went from watching *Parks and Rec* in his bed to watching the *Friends* DVDs I had on constant repeat in my hospital room. We went from engaging in conversations with one another to comforting each other through the silence filled with pain.

I remember, early on after I woke up, the doctors were monitoring my breathing. I was still on a breathing tube, so I had to teach myself what was automatic before…take a breath in, let it out, then repeat the process. It sounds so easy it's silly…but this was my new struggle. I would think of strategies to help reteach myself how to breathe because remember, I couldn't talk to anyone, so really, I was left with a lot of my own thoughts. I remember lying there, my head resting on Jeremy's chest while he was lying close next to me. I could no longer move my neck, so our eyes never caught the gaze of each other. Both lying there in what was our new normal. Just silently thinking. Well, at least thinking on my part; Jeremy could have been sleeping. Both of us were just…there. As I lay there, I would focus on my breaths. I would try and line them up with Jeremy's. I could hear his breath in match up with the feeling of his chest puffing up with air, and I would challenge myself: *Ok Mol, match your breaths with his. Breathe in, breathe out, breathe in*…this would continue until I dozed off. Clearly it worked. Soon after in the days that followed, the doctors decided to try taking me off the breathing machine and letting me breathe on my own through the night. As nights became more regular, we would see if I could manage all day as well as night. Soon, they could put a red cap on the tube that was poking out of my neck. (They didn't remove the tube right away in case I needed it; this way they wouldn't have to do another surgery to place it again.) Today, a deep scar remains in the place my breathing tube was and serves as a reminder to me of what times were like before. Of how the most simple and automatic necessities were a conscious effort to me. Jeremy's breath was one thing I could grasp onto. A world in which everything that was normal to me was suddenly spinning out of control. His breath was the tether thrown out into the dark abyss for me to grasp onto. And luckily, I found it and held on for dear life. It grounded me. Gave me something to focus on and build my successes from there. I will forever be so grateful for that. His breath saved me. He breathed life back into me.

CHAPTER FOUR—
THE GIRL IN A COMA

Being in a coma is extremely hard to describe. It's like trying to describe a dream but when you're saying it out loud, you're realizing the details make no sense. The memories you do have seem so vivid and familiar in your head, but when you try to put them into words, they seem so foreign and blurry. Most of my coma I don't even remember…and I don't try to remember, either. I guess I would spastically sit up then lie back down a lot. I did this all the time. I would kick around in my bed so my legs were riddled with bruises from my thrashing around. Jeremy cut up pool noodles to cover the bars of the bed railings to serve as padding, absorbing most of the brunt in the collision between my legs and the metal bars. There was a time that my flailing got so violent I fell out of my bed…a huge no-no for a brain injured patient. I don't remember any of that. I only know that's what it was like through the stories my mom and Jeremy have told me. My memories I have while I was in a coma are from when I was in the third hospital, Craig Hospital. This was when I was in a semi-conscious state of mind. My eyes were open, but I wasn't responding to anything or anyone; I had no purposeful movement. Jeremy says, "The lights were on but no one was home." I would also, involuntarily, spastically sit up and lie back down. I can't help but think of how scary this must've been for my mom and Jeremy. I was more like the girl from *The Exorcist* rather than the peaceful looking Sleeping Beauty. To me, I knew I was in the hospital, but I didn't know exactly what had happened. Kind of like you know the sky is blue, but you can't explain the exact reasoning of it. At this point I wasn't communicating with doctors or therapists, so doctors weren't asking me "Do you know where you are? Do you know why you're here?", because I wasn't responsive. I was basically a vegetable hooked up to multiple machines, some of which told the outside world I was still alive—reading and tracking my heartbeat, my blood pressure, and my temperature. But without those machines I was basically dead to the world.

I may have been brain-dead to the outside world, but I was a secret observer from the inside, unable to interject my comments. I knew 7:00 a.m. was the nurses' shift change, the switch from night nurses to day nurses. I came to know which nurses and nursing assistants worked well with each other and which ones didn't. I knew the "gossip" because nurses and nursing assistants would talk amongst each other like I wasn't there…because I was "room 317" to them: the girl in the coma. Don't get me wrong, I had great nurses. All did their job and did what they needed to do. I had a couple of nurses who went above and beyond. They talked to me like I was still there, like I was a friend. I'll forever love those nurses. (Ambyr, Molly, Suzie, Joey… I'm talking about you.) My daily routine looked a bit like this:

6:30 a.m. - blood draws and vitals (temperature, blood

pressure, and blood oxygen levels).

7:30-8:00 a.m. - breakfast and morning meds bolus (bolus means being fed through a tube).

12:00 p.m. - lunch bolus.

5:00 p.m. - dinner bolus.

7:30/8:00 p.m. - Jeremy came to spend the night with me.

Then it starts all over the next day.

My days consisted of a lot of nothing. My room was about ten feet by ten feet, with a bathroom attached to it. It was big enough for my bed, that uncomfortable chair all hospital rooms have to serve as a bed to the reluctant guests, and a TV that hung on the wall opposite of the bed. I broke my neck and needed a spinal fusion from the occipital joint of C1 down to C6, requiring a plate that would attach my skull to my spine. The second vertebra is responsible for turning your neck, kind of like a ball and socket joint. Now that that's fused to the vertebrae above and below it, I can't turn my neck. My room had a window in it that allowed the light in from behind my head. Not only was I unable to turn my head to see out the window that was behind me, but I was also lying down, unable to balance and sit myself up. My world was confined to staring at the whiteboard that hung on the wall in front of me. I was also in a type of bed that locked patients in to prevent any falls like I experienced in the previous hospital. The walls that trapped me in the bed were padded so I wouldn't hurt myself when I kicked an arm or leg. Think of a padded cell that you would see in a psychiatric hospital. One friend brought pictures for me and hung them on the bed frame, so when I was conscious, I would have a picture of a beach to look at. She knew my love of ramen so she printed out a picture of a hot bowl of noodles with steam rising up from them ever so gently, yet so thick you could almost taste the broth. She also printed out a picture of me and all my friends when we went out to brunch for my twenty-sixth birthday. There was also a picture of Jeremy and me on New Year's Eve. I remember staring at that picture just thinking to myself...*Only five more hours 'til Jeremy gets here...only four more hours 'til Jeremy gets here...only three more hours 'til Jeremy gets here...only two more hours 'til he gets here...only one more hour 'til Jeremy gets here," until he got there.* Counting down the hours was the only thing I had to occupy my time. In a situation filled with black holes, it was the one silver lining I could manifest. I couldn't even let him know I was happy he was there once he arrived. I was trapped in my own body, screaming on the inside: *I'M STILL HERE! I NEED YOU!* But I was just "room 317" to everyone in the outside world. I was just the girl in a coma.

Then, one night I experienced the sense of being scared. Jeremy was asleep next to me, but I still wasn't talking at this time. A night nurse came in my room because the door cracked open allowing a thin, bright, orange sliver of light to abruptly break the black sea of darkness that had filled the room before. I could see a black silhouette walk in my room and peruse the counter across the room. I thought, *Oh shit, where's my purse?! I hope they don't steal anything.* Now, thinking back on it, of course I didn't have a purse or belongings, because I was in the hospital. Nonetheless, it was an automatic worry. Not that I could react even if I did have belongings. Then it hit me, I was stuck in this semi-conscious state of mind. If someone were to be robbing my hospital room, I couldn't do anything about it. I couldn't stop them. If I couldn't even wake up Jeremy, who was sleeping right next to me, I sure as hell couldn't yell for a nurse to come to my rescue. The feeling of helplessness was so terrifying that even if I could have moved, it wouldn't have mattered because I was scared to stillness. You know how they say you have a moment of flight or fight? There's a third one that's not talked about: freeze. I'm a freeze type of person. The mysterious shadow left the room but my heartbeat must have triggered a machine because a nurse came in after that and turned the lights on to check on me. After she checked all my vitals and saw I was ok, she clicked a button on the machine to stop the beeping, turned the lights off, closed the door, and went back to the nurses' station. Then, like clockwork, 6:30 a.m. came and it was time for morning bloodwork and Jeremy to leave for work.

Another vague, dream-like memory I have is of a suction-machine-thingy I had on my bed, similar to the little wand used at the dentist's office to get the spit. There was one of those that hung on one of the walls at the foot of my bed. It was constantly on and therefore a tiny amount of air was being suctioned through it when it wasn't in use. This caused it to make a tiny, little, mouse-like noise. One day, my mom and sister were sitting in my bed with me and they overheard the annoying sound and started to wonder what the heck that sound was. They laughed at each other, saying, "I'm not crazy right?! What THE HECK is that noise???" They didn't know it was the suction wand that hung at the foot of my bed, but I did. I knew, but I was in my coma so at this point I still wasn't communicating with the outside world. This is one of the memories that I remember so vividly I can almost *feel* it. I felt trapped. I *knew* the mouse-like rustling sound was the suction wand. I also *knew* that information was the missing piece wanted by others, but I couldn't say anything. I *wanted* so badly to fill them in and let them know I had the answer, but I physically couldn't. Later, when I was out of my coma and released from the hospital, I brought up this instance with my mom to see if this really, indeed, did happen. And she yelled in disbelief, "I remember that! That *did* happen!"

That's a memory I have of *before* my consciousness was known to the outside world…when consciousness was a secret that I yearned to reveal. But a memory I will NEVER forget, and one that I hold so close to my heart, is the moment I felt *seen*. Sure, I had a physical appearance the whole time…I knew my body was visible to doctors, family members, and friends, and my eyes were even open giving a stale performance of consciousness, but really there was nothing I could do to prove my existence. There was nothing I could do to prove I was more than just my physical body and a blank stare, more than just the eighty-nine pounds of flesh lying in a hospital bed. My memory of the first time someone saw me as more than that—the first time someone saw me as a thinking, breathing, feeling, human being—is one I hold with Jeremy. And what's even more satisfying, is that this moment can be confirmed by Jeremy, because he remembers it exactly the same way as I do. He remembers it as me being me for the first time.

I had been in a semi-conscious state of mind for months now. We got in the swing of things, our new normal. Whether we got used to it or not didn't matter…it was there, it was our new life. One day, we were doing our regular thing to pass the hours by in the day. Jeremy was helping move me around to provide gentle stretches to my bedbound body. Like I said before, I was not a sleeping beauty coma patient. I rarely lay motionless—I was always moving and shifting about involuntarily. Oftentimes nurses would come in and joke about how I must have "abs of steel" because of my incessant sitting up/lying down. Again, these aren't conversations had WITH me, rather they're comments I observed while nurses made their rounds. I was like a fly on the wall. In this instance, while Jeremy was stretching me, I abruptly sat up and Jeremy said, "Whoa, girl! Stop showing off! We're not doing V-ups!" And I laughed: one, because the thought of a comatose patient showing off is ridiculous, and two, because "V-ups" was a new term to me. Everyone had mentioned something about me and my SIT-UPS but not V-ups. When I laughed a sound came out that the rest of the world could hear. Before that, I could *think about* laughing, screaming, or crying but it didn't matter, I couldn't get my body to produce a noise. I remember, for so long, wanting SO BADLY for a sound, a look…anything. I wanted my body to give any sort of sign that could serve as a connection to the outside world and something to tell them I was still here and desperately trying. I needed that connection so people wouldn't give up on me. I was in such a state of desperation for so long that it started to turn into hopelessness. So when Jeremy made the V-ups comment, I wasn't even trying to make a noise when I laughed because I had nearly given up on being noticed. When I laughed it caught me off guard just as much as it caught Jeremy off guard. He gave me that look of bewilderment. A look of *What just happened?!? Did you really just laugh?!* Then he smiled and laughed along with me while giving me a hug. I still couldn't talk but in our silent embrace I knew he saw me. He knew I was still there. I had made my one connection I'd been yearning for months. Jeremy had satisfied my most important craving, my craving for life, for human connection. I'm so grateful it was with him, too…I have all the faith that he'll never give up on me.

Another memory that I'd like to think is uniquely bizarre is one of my surgeries that I endured. This was after I was discharged from the hospital and living at my parents' house, so it wasn't an emergency surgery, rather an outpatient, elective surgery. It was a surgery to help my vocal cords function properly in making my voice loud enough to hear. The surgeon would place a piece of silicon behind the vocal cord to move it over so when the working cord did its job, it would have something to vibrate against and make noise, thus giving me my voice back. The only thing: my response was needed to determine how far to push the vocal cord over. This meant I had to be awake throughout the surgery. The doctors promised me I wouldn't feel anything more than a slight tug, but they said they couldn't use drugs to knock me out because they needed me to say "ahh" to see if the movement was enough for the other chord to hit it. It was such an outlandish experience. I grew up watching the medical dramas like *ER* and *Grey's Anatomy*, and now I was living it. I was the patient who had to be awake as they sliced my throat open.

I was wheeled into the operating room and transferred, head up, to the operating table. There was a nurse, the surgeon, and the anesthesiologist in the room. The surgeon reassured me that I wouldn't feel any pain, but I was going to be awake. He then placed a sheer piece of cloth on my head that had the opacity of a shower curtain. He said he was going to do this so he could place his tools in a more comfortable spot for his reach rather than on a tray to the side of him. Then he started his incision which would stretch from one ear to the other about an inch below my jaw line. Once he had my throat cut open he said, "You ok, Molei? I have the first cut done." I whispered back, "Yup." It was truly so odd thinking, *I know I should be in pain. A 2½ inch gash was just made, exposing the inside of my throat to the world, and yet I feel **nothing**.* I remember seeing the outline of the scalpel lying on the sheet that covered my face and determining, "Ok, that's the scalpel," but I couldn't figure out what the orangish-red blob was that was next to it. It didn't hold the shape of any medical tools that I was familiar with and even if it did, I questioned if they made scalpels/tweezers/ gauze in different colors. Then it hit me: the orangish-red blob was the insides of my throat. I just thought, *Is this really happening. Is this really my life??* Then the surgeon said, "Ok Molei, the silicone is in…now it's just a matter of seeing how far to move your vocal cord over—can you say 'ahhh' for me?" I said "ahh" but a gasp of air muted my voice. He said, "Ok, let me move it over some more." He finagled my throat some more and asked again, "Ok, try now." Again, nothing more than an incredibly breathy whisper escaped. At this point I was feeling so defeated. I knew that going into this surgery didn't guarantee my voice to return but I had such high hopes. He fiddled with my vocal cords again and asked me one last time, "Ok, try now." This time, to my surprise, it wasn't the breathy gasp of air but an actual sound. It wasn't a loud one, but it wasn't the exasperated waste of air I was used to. It was more like the sound of someone mumbling under their breath. Still, the results weren't up to my expectations; but it was more than I came in with. He said, "That's our magic spot! I'm gonna close you back up and we'll be all done." He stitched me up and I was wheeled to the post-op area. I just remember being so thirsty. It was as if I was roaming the hot Saharan Desert for weeks without water, and the post-op room had my glass of crisp, cold water. But there was one major complication standing in the way of my relief. In order to quench the agonizing thirst that overcame me, one must know how to swallow. It's such a simple and basic task it sounds ridiculous saying, but I still didn't know how to swallow. I still had my feeding tube because eating and drinking were still things to be learned for me. I was learning them but it was just a long process for me and, at the time, I was still using quite a bit of thickener[2]. Due to my inability to swallow, the best they could do was give me water-soaked cotton balls to suck on. That is the most tortuous memory I have; not the being awake part. The unquenchable thirst.

I have memories of surgeries, like that one, that make me look like the bad-ass patient, but I also have memories of smaller surgeries. The surgery that brought me the most pride in getting through it was a small surgery in comparison to all the other surgeries I've had. It's not even a surgery that required scalpels; it was the removal of a

---

[2] Thickener is a substance used to change the consistency of your liquid. It's often used by people with dysphagia or older individuals. "Thickened liquids give you better control of the liquid in your mouth." ulhc.org

breathing tube. Back before my surgery to fix my vocal cord, the ENT tried a less invasive approach. The thought or intention was to use an injection (similar to Botox) to swell my vocal cord, ultimately making it bigger so the other cord had something to hit, giving me a voice. This involved me going to the ENT's office and getting stabbed with a giant needle directly through my throat and into my vocal cord. He guided a camera through my nasal passage to my throat, which allowed him to ensure he was injecting the right spot. Everything went as planned and I was told not to expect results right away, so I went home with high hopes that the next morning I would just wake up to a voice. About two days post-injection, as I was drinking my green juice (I remember the green juice specifically because it has a thicker consistency, more like a smoothie, so I could drink it without adding thickener to it), and all of the sudden I couldn't get air into my lungs. With each gasp I tried to take, it was as if the air was hitting a brick wall, causing me to cough. My mom ran over to me and asked if I was ok, to which I frantically looked at her and shook my head, letting her know I was NOT ok. She asked me, "Should I call 911?", to which I widened my eyes indicating "YES." The ambulance came and I was rushed to the hospital. I heard the EMT say he was having difficulties finding a vein—which came as no surprise to me because of the repeated failed attempts in finding a good vein for my morning blood draws, which left my arms bruised resembling a drug addict's used-up arm. I don't remember much of my arrival at the hospital, except they put a mask on me that forcefully pushed air into my mouth. I remember it being frantic, and through the hustle and bustle of all the nurses and doctors pushing my bed to an operating room I remember thinking, *Where is he!? I need to see Jeremy before I go in the room.* As my eyes were frantically scanning the many faces that were in my view, I felt someone grab my hand. I followed the arm up to see Jeremy kissing my hand, reassuring me it'd be alright. I immediately felt a sense of relief. I'm not trying to be dramatic about this experience, but I can honestly say that I felt at ease as soon as I saw Jeremy's face. I thought, *Ok…whatever happens will happen. I'm ok now that I saw him.* I know that sounds as if I thought I was dying and I was desperately searching for the love of my life in my final moments on this Earth, but for me, in that moment, that's exactly how I felt. I've never felt so scared for my life as I felt in that moment. The next thing I remember is waking up in the ICU with the unnerving feeling that a load of bricks was on top of my arms. I couldn't move them to scratch my nose. I quickly realized they were tied to the sides of the bed in order to keep me from yanking the tube that was inserted down my throat to help me breathe. Turns out, being conscious and intubated at the same time is incredibly bothersome and it's an automatic reaction to reach and yank it out, but that can cause devastating effects on the airway; hence the arm restraints. The injection in my vocal cord had caused an adverse reaction causing my airway walls to swell up, which in turn inhibited my ability to breathe. It caused my airways to collapse, thus dramatically decreasing the space for air to move to and from my lungs. I spent two nights in the ICU with a tube down my throat and under observation. Being intubated and conscious *is*, in fact, one of the worst feelings. It was extremely uncomfortable, and not to mention, I couldn't use my arms because they were tied to the bed. You also can't talk when you're intubated, so imagine just lying in a hospital bed with a tube hanging out of your mouth not being able to do anything. You can't even wipe the drool dripping out of your mouth because the tube prevents mobilization of your tongue and lips. You can't use a tissue to wipe the snot that's running out of your nose because the restraints are holding your arms down making them useless. I truly felt helpless (at least when I was in my coma state people didn't know I was there on the inside…now I was visibly conscious but something was inhibiting my communication). My cousin and his son came to visit me but I couldn't say anything back to them. My friend from high school worked at the hospital I was in and came by my room, but I couldn't reminisce with her and tell her how much I appreciated her coming to visit me because I had a stupid tube in my mouth. On the third day the doctor said the swelling had gone down and it was time to remove the tube, but he warned me this was about to be a very uncomfortable experience. He told me they had to do it in an operating room even though the removal process didn't involve any cutting into me. If I couldn't get my breath under control, they'd have to take desperate measures and trach me again. That means all my hard work of relearning how to breathe on my own would go for nothing. If I had to be re-trached I would have nothing to show for my hard work. The doctor told me it was going to be extremely uncomfortable, and it was even slightly painful. I was going to uncontrollably cough and have a hard time finding my breath, but he told me to really focus on taking a breath in then letting it out. When I recall his warning, I'm surprised it didn't scare me shitless, but I remember thinking, *Ok, I'm gonna need you to be patient with me. Don't rush and cut into my trachea erasing all my hard work. Just give me a chance to find my breath and I will. I promise!* I swear I conveyed that message to him but now, thinking back on it, I had no way of communicating. Nonetheless, I felt we were on the same wavelength. The procedure was nothing more than him and another doctor standing by me as one of them carefully and slowly pulled the tube out. I remember thinking, *Just yank it out quick!*, because the slow-moving tube was causing my gag reflex to react along with the violent cough the surgeon warned me about. It was such a strong and heavy cough it felt like someone was punching all the air out of me by hitting me in the back with each cough I let out. At the end of each cough I found myself desperately gasping for air before the next cough came. Then I remembered the surgeon telling me to focus on one breath. *Take a breath in…then let it out.* After, what seemed like forever, I finally found a rhythm. Breathe in, breathe out. I opened my eyes and looked around the room to see the two doctors smiling at me and encouraging me, saying, "Good job, Molei. There ya go! In…out…in…out." I remember feeling like I just did the impossible. I just cheated death, *yet again.* I barely missed landing on the "go back to start" space. I was not going to have to be re-trached and put back on a ventilator. They rolled me back to my room where they watched me for a few hours to make sure I was alright and then I was discharged to go back home. To this day, I hear Sia's song, "Alive," and can't help but feel like that song was made with me in mind. The lyrics are: "Took it all, but I'm still breathing" but I hear: "Took it **out,** but I'm still breathing" (referring to my breathing tube).

CHAPTER FIVE-
CRAIG HOSPITAL

Being a rehabilitation hospital, Craig Hospital in Denver, Colorado isn't like normal hospitals. Or I guess I should say it's not what I would associate with hospitals. There's no hustle and bustle of nurses running from room to room. There's no waiting area packed with potential patients sitting eagerly waiting to hear their names called like they're the winner of a raffle. It doesn't even look like a hospital from the outside. However, there is the distant sound of ambulance sirens because next door is an emergency hospital. Otherwise, those who aren't familiar with Craig wouldn't even be aware it's a hospital. It doesn't look like what I think of when I hear the word hospital. I think of harshly lit, sterile halls with rooms closely crammed next to each other on either side of the hall. Don't get me wrong, Craig has the jarring fluorescent lights and the uninviting smell of disinfectant but when you look down the halls you may see a patient working with their therapist on walking. Or you may see another patient catching a beach ball thrown by their physical therapist as their exercise to work on their reaction time. Maybe you'd see a patient trying to propel themselves in their newly fitted wheelchair. It's full of progress that's visible which I'm sure is the reason why I always tell people, "As corny as it sounds, it really is a magical place."

Craig consists of two buildings: East and West. East is mostly patient family housing since they have injured people from all over the United States to get some of the best rehabilitation therapy for Traumatic Brain Injuries (TBIs) and Spinal Cord Injuries (SCIs). Luckily, I was only there for two months and my family lives in Colorado, so I didn't have much need to go to the East building. The West building has four floors. When you walk in through the front door, you're welcomed by someone sitting at the front desk. To the left is a small waiting area usually occupied by patients stoically waiting for their rides or passively passing time between outpatient therapy sessions. To the right is the Peak Center which is a recreation center that includes many high-tech machines, along with the regular work-out machines you see in any 24-Hour Fitness. The third floor is for the TBI patients and the fourth floor houses the SCI patients. I don't know what's on the second floor and now that I think of it, as often as I was at Craig, I never went to the second floor. My world was confined to the third floor, room 317. Most of my therapy (speech, occupational, and physical) were in different rooms on the third floor but it's hard to find differences between them. One of my early challenges was to instruct the nurse which way to go as she pushed me to my daily therapy. This was a way to test the part of the brain that's responsible for direction. My mom and Jeremy laughed and told the nurses I've *always* been directionally challenged. Anyone who knows me knows I'm *terrible* with directions. Regardless to what my navigational skills were before the accident, I was no exception to the rule;

that part of the brain was injured so it still needed rehabilitating.

The doctors and nurses at Craig do such a great job at making sure a patient's world isn't refrained to the 120 square foot by 140 square foot space that is their room. They have numerous reasons for patients to leave their room, like patient outings for those patients well enough to leave the hospital. But honestly, I have never been much of the social butterfly. I found small talk tedious and not worth the effort for the returns I got. I've often thought, *It's a good thing I have my girls otherwise I'd have no friends* (because of my terrible social skills and my preference for the ease that comes with being anti-social). When I first arrived at Craig I was in a coma, so patient outings weren't an option for me. Eventually I woke up and I was well enough to earn my patient-outings, but I'd often decline them, telling the nurse the day of that I didn't feel like an outing. Having the fortunate benefit of hindsight, I now see how my refusal of reintegration help must have made my nurses feel like I was a lost cause. They can't *force patients* to go on outings and have a good time. One thing they could do was make my therapy sessions group-oriented. Some therapy was one-on-one but others were held in group classes filled with fellow inpatients. For those classes you'd have a "companion" accompany you to help you in the event you need any. Even those sessions, they wouldn't force you to go to or stay the entirety.

One specific group therapy session I recall, we were doing easy exercises with TheraBands that offered VERY little resistance. I couldn't help but picture the older lady on PBS who does "workouts" all while sitting in a chair, ya know…meant for older people.…I kept thinking, *THIS is what my life has come to!* My companion that day was a longtime friend, she is actually the first friend I've ever had. We measure our friendship in decades rather than years. We were both on the varsity volleyball team in high school and yet there we were, two varsity volleyball players, performing a simple task that most able-bodied people would consider a stretch. But to me, at that very moment in time, that was a challenge.

I remember a girl in my class wasn't having it-she wanted nothing to do with the class. She would yell in her frustrations. The first outburst caught the class by surprise with all participants staring with their eyes but not daring to turn their heads to make their attention obvious. By the second and third outburst, her companion asked her, "Do you want to go back to your room?" and they left. I remember thinking, *I'm pretty sure that's not allowed,* as if we were in school and she was ditching class. That was the moment that it hit me: my recovery is up to **me.** From the moment I woke up from my coma, my life and its well-being were in the hands of the doctors and nurses. I had no say in what was happening in my life. The doctor said I needed a CAT scan so I got a CAT scan. The hospital said visiting hours were over so no more visitors allowed. I didn't even have a say in what I ate because I couldn't eat solids so I was being tube fed. The part that involves taste and opinions was being skipped so I got what was in the hospitals inventory of bolus slush (Bolus was the term used for my tube-fed meals). I was at the complete mercy of the nurses and doctors around me. And while that's true in a lot of senses; ultimately, it was my decision to participate in therapies. I made a conscious choice and silently promised to myself that I will do everything on my part to help them (the nurses and doctors) do their job in getting me better. That's the moment when I started looking at us as a team; we were all working on getting the old-Molei back. I'm so, incredibly grateful and I count my blessings that I got the best teammates to ever exist. I had the absolute best doctors, the cream of the crop nurses, the most patient and dedicated therapists, the nicest and most caring CNAs, I even made sure to let the janitorial staff know that I appreciated them coming and cleaning my room daily.

It wasn't until about a month after I got to Craig that I woke from my coma and could participate in therapies. Once that happened, my days consisted of:

Therapy.

Sleeping.

Therapy.

Eating.

And more therapy.

Each week I would get a schedule of my itinerary telling me which therapy I was scheduled in. But first, each day would start with *ADLs*. ADL stands for activities of daily life. An occupational therapist would come spend the first thirty minutes of my scheduled days helping me get ready for the day; we would work on things like brushing my teeth or putting on my shirt. Those two things usually took me the full thirty minutes so we only got that far but for other patients I'm sure they did things like washing their face and putting pants on. At that time, those tasks were too advanced for me, I barely had enough balance to keep myself sitting upright, let alone stand. So I stuck with the tasks that didn't require any standing or balancing.

Next, the nurse would come in with my morning bolus. I usually had ten to fifteen minutes before my first scheduled therapy session because the act of chewing and swallowing your food takes more time than it takes for the milky slush to be pushed through a tube into your stomach. Being unable to eat played well for my anti-social tendencies because I never had to go to the cafeteria, where I had the chance of mingling with other inpatients. There was no dining with others for my meals. It was just me, my mom or Jeremy and the nurse administering the day's bolus.

My day's schedule usually included speech therapy, physical therapy or occupational therapy on it. Speech therapy obviously works on your speech but it also consists of cognitive therapy as well. My first, most obvious deficit was speaking *anything.* Dysarthria isn't an uncommon diagnosis for many of the patients. According to Mayoclinic.org, dysarthria is a condition in which the muscles you use for speech are weak or you have difficulty controlling them. Aphasia is also a common occurrence. The Mayo Clinic defines it as a condition that robs you of the ability to communicate. If you've ever heard someone use the phrase "It's on the tip of my tongue..." that's the best description I can give you to relate to what's happening. I knew I *knew* the word...it was a common word I used every day...but for some reason I was just having a *brain fart.* I was blanking at the moment...but the thing was, it wasn't just a moment's time. When I first came across my first bout of aphasia I thought, *This is so weird! It'll come to me in a second...* But it never came. Have you ever seen an actor in a TV show and thought, *What movie are they in? I swear I just saw them...*? It's hard to focus on the TV show you're currently watching because you can't stop obsessing on the question. You start going through each TV show you just watched, maybe you try and remember who you were with to try and narrow your results down, until FINALLY! The lightbulb switches on and you find out what it is that you watched that had the actor. You breathe a huge sigh of relief and allow your brain to go back to enjoying the show. Imagine never being able to breathe the sigh of relief, the light never turns on. You're always stuck in that frustrating space of almost recalling…it's on the tip of your tongue. That's the feeling that aphasia leaves its victims with. I can remember being so frustrated it would bring me to tears. I don't know how or why my aphasia went away but I'm so glad it did. Whenever I interact with a less fortunate person who is still in the grip of aphasia, I feel so bad for them I want to cry. I'm immediately brought back to the frustration of wanting to just communicate with the outside world. My aphasia mainly happened when I was in inpatient speech therapy. When I first awoke, I couldn't speak so the first huge battle was finding a way to communicate. The speech therapists noticed I kicked my right foot a lot as I was sitting in the wheelchair so she somehow conveyed that a horizontal movement with my foot meant "no" and a vertical motion meant "yes." How she got this accomplished, I don't know, because my neck is fused so I can't turn my neck side to side like one does when shaking their head no and I can't nod my head up and down indicating yes. Even in the slight chance I got the opportunity to steal a slight movement, I was in a giant neck collar whose stiffness and rigidity held a strict watch over any movements.

Then I moved up to what I refer to as "the Orange Box days." The Orange Box was simply a square cut-out, made of orange construction paper with the words "yes" and "no" written on the top and bottom of it. It was meant for a way of communication with me. Whoever was speaking to me could hold the box to frame their face and then they could ask me yes or no questions. If the answer was yes, I'd look at "yes" which was on the top side of the frame; similarly, if the answer was no I'd look at "no" at the bottom of the frame. This helped tremendously because now I could be asked, "Are you in pain?" or "Are you hungry?"

The first night I started using this Orange Box, my best girlfriend, Bayle, came to visit me, and Jeremy explained how to use it; we finally had our first conversation post-accident. This will always be a moment I hold close in my heart. Bayle asked me, "Do you know where you are?" I looked up for yes. "Do you know we all love you?" Again, I looked up. "Do you know it's May 2016?" My eyes shot up. "Are you in physical pain right now?" My eyes went down for no. "Are you getting annoyed of me asking you all these questions?" THAT question I'll always remember. It was like I could joke around again. It was a sense of normalcy in this unfamiliar world I was forced to live in. I looked at "no" while laughing inside. I spent about a week using the Orange Box, then I graduated to a DynaVox speech generating machine. A speaking machine that could use my eye gaze and a computer screen to communicate with the outside world. The screen would pop up with boxes that had phrases like "I feel" or "I want." It would then track my eye gaze and if I stared at an option long enough it would advance to another screen with more options like "sad," "mad," "cold," "warm," "water," "food," "blanket." My stare was the same as double-clicking. The machine would speak in a robotic voice my choices, if I stared at "I feel" and "cold" it would announce to the world: I. Feel. Cold. I only remember using this device when I was in speech therapy because it requires setting it up to a computer to use it. It wasn't as easy as grabbing a cut-out lying by the side of the bed.

In my vague memories, it wasn't long before I started talking. But when I did start talking it was nothing more than a faint whisper and my breath control was so weak I could only speak three words per breath. When I was trached after the accident, the insertion of the tube paralyzed a vocal cord. In order to produce sound, you push air past your vocal cords, which then causes them to vibrate against each other producing sound. Since one of my vocal cords is paralyzed, it could no longer move, leaving the other vocal cord stranded. The vocal cord needs something to bounce against to reverberate any sound. With only one working cord, I was left with an exasperated huff of a sound for a voice. After being left with a faint whisper for a voice, we worked on communicating with what I had. I was taught to think of the best way to get my point across with the least amount of words. Example: If I want to say, "I would like a glass of water, please," that's eight words. I could only get out four per breath so I had to think how to chop that down. I was constantly strategizing; I was taught to think which words were the most important and is there another way to say it? I found in a lot of cases; manners go out the window. Manners require more words. In the previous example of wanting a glass of water: "Can I have water" is the winner—only four words…no more "please" or "thank you."

Another "class" I became a frequent visitor in was physical therapy. I like to say, of the three therapies (speech, occupational, and physical) physical therapy is the "favorite child." Those are the things you learn how to do that the outside world *wants* to see. In my news stories, they wanted the shot of me taking my first steps or learning how to ski again, not the exercises working on the muscles in my throat like I did in speech or the fine motor muscle movements I worked on in occupational therapy. Picture a scene with the snow-packed ground rushing by, and as the camera pans out you see a wobbly, disabled girl working hard to keep her balance. (I'm referring to the news story that followed me during my first skiing trip post-accident.) That makes for a better scene rather than me sitting in my family room with my occupational therapist as I struggle, holding the small disc in my fingers all while contemplating where to drop my next piece in Connect Four. Not exactly the most captivating stuff yet just as important. I agree that physical therapy is much more exciting to watch (if you're bored enough to watch it in the first place). When I first started going to physical therapy we were working on mind-numbingly easy stuff like balance. A specific balance test I did often was the Berg Balance test. It's a series of different exercises or activities to test your balance. For example, one of the timed events is going from a seated position to a standing one ten times. One task is turning around 360 degrees—the therapist would even demonstrate it first in case your knowledge on how many degrees a circle comprises is lagging. Then, if I could turn in a full circle, I would attempt it with my eyes closed. It's an easy test to say the least. On each task the physical therapist would judge me on my performance; how was my gait? Did I stumble or fall? If it was a timed question—how long did it take me to complete it? Did I complete it? The test is out of fifty-six points. The first time I took it I got a six...single digit, SIX. Upon learning my results, I immediately thought, *Well, my physical therapist must not like me! She's such a goody-two-shoes anyway, she must need everything perfect to give it any score. Whatever...I know I'm not a six!* I took that test again, two years later in my outpatient therapy class, and I realized I really was a six. Even when I took it the second time, I still only got a forty-eight, and even that was being generous. It wasn't until I had the benefit of hindsight to see that I was, in fact, only a six.

The third therapy to round out my daily therapies was occupational therapy. Before this all happened, had you asked me what occupational therapy was, I would have guessed "something to do with one's occupation." I had no idea what occupational therapy was (or as it's referred to in the hospital, OT) I quickly learned it's the everyday activities we take for granted. It's tying your shoes or the fine motor movements required in using a pencil to write your name. In my case, writing was way too advanced. My occupational therapy consisted of me working on a puzzle and all the fine motor movements that come with reaching for the piece and meticulously arranging it to fit. A major challenge of mine was working on a puzzle while standing the entire time. (With the therapist standing close by, of course, to catch me if I fell).

In one of the sessions my brother was accompanying me and he brought his eight-year-old son. His son had a toy car with him to satisfy his mind's relentless need for amusement, which wasn't uncommon for an eight-year-old. As we started the session and the therapist was explaining to me the challenge for the day, my brother had to keep shushing his son whenever he let his imagination run too wild and he found himself involved in a high-speed chase with the toy car. At each scold, his son would quiet down but soon after, his imagination would flare up and car noises would come barreling out of his mouth with his hands making the car do back flips and tipsy turns. He was so captivated in his play that he lost balance and fell off his chair. My brother quickly and fiercely shot a look of death to him to sit down and behave while his son quickly and quietly muddled an apology. I just remember bursting out in laughter. His son looked at me with confusion trying to figure out if he was in trouble or if he was the comedian in the room. He chose to play off my reaction and started laughing too.

My days were filled with therapies so having a visitor attend one while visiting me wasn't uncommon and, if I'm being honest, it was something I had to get used to quickly once therapies became a part of my life. After all, I was in a rehab hospital, to be a patient there you have to prove you can be there. Back when I was in the first two hospitals, I was non-responsive to any commands given to me. Nurses would test my awareness by asking me to track things with my eyes. "Molei, if you can hear me…follow my finger?" They would also hold my hand and say "Molei, if you can hear me, squeeze my hand." They would come in daily, poking and prodding me, and I wouldn't respond. It came to be a deflating routine for my mom: the nurses would come in, pinch me, tell me to squeeze a hand if I was there, and then, with no response from me, they would leave and come back to test my existence the next day. One morning, the nurse, Kat, came in and said her morning greetings to my mom—the nursing staff became like extended family to my mom as she saw them daily for weeks at a time. She began to do the daily test of my awareness. She pinched my arms and legs and told me to track her finger with my eyes. With my usual non-responsive reaction, she moved on to the next test and grabbed my hands and told me to squeeze if I could hear her. To much of her surprise she felt a squeeze. My mom says Kat looked back in complete shock and with tears in her eyes. From that moment a new goal of mine was to show purposeful movement so I could get into Craig Hospital. (Craig Hospital is a rehabilitation hospital serving patients well enough to be rehabilitated. A comatose patient won't get much benefit out of it if they're unresponsive and in a coma.) Doctors would give me different orders to obey, like moving a finger when the held up my wrist in the air. If I did it that would serve as proof that I was in there and able to get the help I desperately needed at Craig. Now that I squeezed Kat's hand to tell her I was in there, I needed to prove to a doctor I was worthy enough for Craig Hospital. That doctor in my story—the one who deserves most (if not all) of the credit for my recovery, the one who *started* my recovery, the one who got me into Craig—was named Dr. Yarnell. Dr. Yarnell is an older gentleman with white hair and a bushy mustache to match. His primary hospital he works in is the first hospital I was brought to, but he followed and checked up on me while I was at Craig. My nurses at Craig knew who he was because he's a loud (not loud in the annoying-drunk-girl-kind of way, but loud in the assured-confident-professional-kind of way)doctor and I'm sure he has many patients who go to Craig. Back when I still needed to prove to a doctor I was well enough to go to Craig, he is a main reason for my admission. My mom tells the story of a doctor holding up my limp and motionless hand and saying, "Molei, move your pointer finger." And when my finger would move *a half of a millimeter*, barely enough for the naked eye to see, he would proclaim "See! Purposeful movement. Get her into Craig!" I picture him letting go of his grip causing my hand to fall to my side. He then whips around with his eyes closed in assurance as he makes his way to his next patient in his morning rounds. I'll never know how this story really played out because I was in a coma, but I like my version I have in my head.

Therapy has had such a big impact on my life to date. Back when I was first discharged from the hospital and living at my parents', I couldn't start outpatient therapy right away because I wasn't well enough to make it a full day being away from home. Being inpatient is different because if you get tired or cranky, as TBI patients often do, someone can just wheel you back to your room. Being outpatient is different because you're no longer living in the hospital. If I got tired or cranky it was not a quick elevator ride back to the third floor. It was a forty-five-minute drive to a different city where my parents lived. That was where home therapy came in. Home therapy is exactly what it sounds like: therapy at your home. A speech therapist, occupational therapist, and physical therapist all came to my home and worked with the objects available to me. For example, I would often use parallel bars in my physical therapy sessions at the hospital, but since I didn't have parallel bars at my parent's house, I would use the banister my parents had. The therapists would bring some items, like my speech therapist brought her electro stimulation device used for stimulating muscles in my throat to help with my swallowing.

Diane, my occupational therapist, would bring games like Connect Four to work on fine motor movements of my hands. She also had me cook a dinner for my family one night. This may not seem like a huge deal but it was a big challenge for me at the time. Not only did I need help standing and walking my way throughout the kitchen, but I had to finagle objects that could do harm to me, like a knife or the stove. There's a lot of cognitive requirements that go unnoticed in simple tasks like measuring out a cup of flour. *First, you must carefully walk to the cupboard. Next, you have to reach and get the flour without losing your balance. Walk back. Now that you have the flour, find your measuring cups and measure out the cup of flour— think, is it best to pour the flour into the cup or use the cup and scoop out the desired amount? Now you need to return the flour.* That may seem like overkill in explaining the process, but I promise you—that is what's going through my mind *in everything I do*. With my brain injury, there's no more simply, "get a cup of flour"....I can get the cup of flour but it's no longer simple. Before the accident, I *did not* enjoy cooking. I lived in the city so there were tons of restaurants within walking distance to me. I had a deli across the street from my apartment and if I needed to make the longer trip to the grocery store, the Safeway was only five blocks away. Basically, my thought was *Why would anyone make their meal when there are tons of restaurants that'll do it for you?* I realize how privileged and snotty that makes me sound but I'm ashamed to say, I've actually said those words. After that night cooking in OT, I made cooking part of my daily therapy. I cook close to every night for Jeremy and myself and I've found a joy in it. I wouldn't say I have a passion for it, but I don't mind cooking for myself like I did before.

My occupational therapist at Craig Hospital would go speak with the graduate students in the Occupational Therapy Program at Colorado State University specifically training to help those with TBIs or SCIs. She would speak to them as a recent graduate and a now employed OT at a prestigious rehabilitation hospital. She asked if I would like to accompany her and speak to the class to give them a perspective of a *patient*. I eagerly accepted and took such honor in being asked. I was able to sit through the lecture and then participate in their lab where we did many things I did in OT. While I was there, I met a student, Carolyn, who was doing her rotations at Craig so she was planning to move to Denver soon. We kept in touch and when she did move, we met up for happy hour. Hers is one of many friendships I value and I don't take it for granted because I know how hard it is to make friends as an adult. I cherish Carolyn's and my friendship so much.

One of the more cumbersome outcomes from the accident was controlling my emotions and what a new struggle it was for me. I had heard the stories and listened to the doctor's warnings to my family and friends that I may not be the 'usual Molei'—that I could get upset easily. They were warned not to be offended or surprised by my behavior and assured that it was because of the brain injury if I was agitated, irritated, or rude.

I would hear these stories and warnings and think, *But that's not me.* I was not willing to be clumped into a group. Being a TBI survivor should be something to be proud of, not a warning. "She has a TBI, so that's why she's so mean," or "She has a TBI, that's why she has no filter." I recognize that a TBI can be the cause of things like that, especially being around so many TBI survivors in Craig, but I didn't feel like that was the case for me. And I still, wholeheartedly, believe that.

I did, however, notice its effect on my emotions, and specifically speaking, controlling them. I had no more poker face and couldn't keep my feelings inside. If my nostrils were suddenly assaulted with an unpleasant smell, you would know by the giant stink face I displayed as if I were acting like a dramatic child. If I saw someone wearing something I wouldn't dare to wear, my judgement was clear as day in my confused look and furled eyebrows. If I caught glimpse of someone almost falling, maybe they caught themselves before they fully fell (that moment we've all had, when we almost trip but don't, then you look around to check if anyone else noticed—yeah **that** moment). If I happened to catch a glimpse of you in this moment chances are, I was laughing. It wasn't with an evil intention but, more so, I find tripping comical, so I laugh.

Not only would I laugh at funny things, but I would find myself laughing at inappropriate times. My hospital bed had giant padded walls on it so they could be shut and prevent me from rolling out of bed. Once I woke from the coma, the doctors and nurses would explain the reason as to why I was in one of these beds. They reiterated the importance in not trying to climb over the walls because I could fall. If I needed to get out, call for help and they'll help me get out, it's not meant to keep me trapped in. When they were telling me this I couldn't help from laughing. I just kept getting a picture in my mind of a twenty-eight-years-old Molei, struggling to climb a hospital bed wall, with my ass hanging out of the hospital gown with a nurse catching glimpse of it on the monitor screen before she comes rushing in. It was a comical view that made me grin from ear to ear with the occasional giggle. But that was not the time to be laughing. It's hard to convey you understand the seriousness of the consequences involved when you're laughing. That's the first time I can recall laughing at an inappropriate time but that's because of my picture that would pop up in my mind. A movie would pop into my head and the scene was a funny one. But laughing would become my go-to reaction, especially in serious times.

Once I was discharged from the hospital and living with my parents', I would be in an argument with my mom and smirking and laughing. I would have to tell her, "I'm sorry I'm laughing. I'm taking this seriously and want to be taken seriously but I don't know why I'm laughing." Laughing came out when I was angry, but it also came out when I was sad.

Shortly after I was discharged from the hospital, my best friend from high school committed suicide and my world was shaken, yet again. I got a text in a group text asking me if I was OK and I remember reading it with such confusion. I quickly scrolled through previous texts to see if I accidentally sent a butt-text, but I didn't, so I responded with, "What are you talking about?" Then another text came through with, "About Patrick. I just heard. I'm so sorry." I wrote back with, "What's up with Patrick? What happened?" I then saw I had a Facebook message from his older brother explaining that Patrick had taken his own life. I read it in complete disbelief. How could this be possible? I had *just* spoken with Patrick and we were planning on him coming out to my parents' house so we could visit. It had been a few years since we saw each other so it would be so nice to hear how our adult lives have been shaping up and taking form. I had scheduled a time but then realized I committed to a time when I had speech therapy. I noticed and texted Patrick, unbeknownst to me, the last time ever. I said, "Patrick, I have to propose a new time for our get together but I swear it's not out of me not wanting to make time for you. I have speech therapy but it's only for an hour...so if you want you can come an hour later. Let me know and I can also give you a refresher on how to make it out to my parents in case you forget how to get here." If I knew that was the last time I'd speak to him I would've said something different. I would've told him how much I love him and how much he meant to me. I was left with so many questions: was he hurting when we texted? What would have our get together been like? Would I have noticed his unhappiness and help him, or would my accident and my new life have taken precedent and hog the majority of the conversation? Those will be questions that will never be answered because Patrick killed himself shortly after. I was too late to help him. It's a burden I will carry the rest of my life or at least every time I see something that makes me think of him...and I think of him often. Patrick's funeral was the first funeral I went to post-accident. Jeremy accompanied me and pushed me in my wheelchair. When I got there the ushers ushered me to a spot where my wheelchair wouldn't be in the way when the pallbearers brought the casket forth. I remember my head felt too heavy to keep up, so I didn't try to fight it. My chin stayed tucked in by my chest and my eyes were staring at the program that had a picture of Patrick vibrantly smiling back at me. I remember having an out-of-body moment and the thought of *Look at where we're at?! This is so ridiculous! This isn't how me and Patrick's lives are supposed to be. This is so stupid!*

And then before I knew it, I was laughing. The first laugh slipped out with me slapping my hand to cover my mouth and suddenly the weight of my head didn't matter because I was quickly scanning my surroundings trying to see if anyone caught my wildly, inappropriate, **rude,** laugh that could easily be seen as a sign of disrespect. I had to use my hands to cup my mouth and hide my grin. I tucked my head back down and tried to play it off as sobs escaping rather than the laughs. Patrick's funeral is a painful memory I have; the fact that we were at Patrick's funeral to begin with, my uncontrollable urge to laugh, the somberness in the air...there's not a thing I like when I think back on that memory. I miss Patrick deeply.

CHAPTER SIX-
A TRUE MILLENNIAL: LIVING AT MY PARENTS' AT AGE TWENTY-NINE

Even though I made big enough strides as an inpatient to prove to doctors I could move on to outpatient care, I wasn't well enough to be living on my own. I required an immense amount of help in everything I did. I hadn't mastered my transfers from my wheelchair yet and thus, I still needed help going to the bathroom. I couldn't shower on my own, I couldn't prepare meals for myself or even grab a glass out of the cupboard without losing my balance. Though I wasn't requiring daily vital checks or blood draws anymore, I was still far away from living independently, which is why I moved back in with my parents. Jeremy had agreed to move in as well to help me in my recovery. This was the first time I'd ever lived with a boy (besides my dad and brother) and believe me when I tell you, this is not the way I thought it would go.

Just to be clear, before the accident, Jeremy and I had

only been together as boyfriend/girlfriend for a very short amount of time. I mean we had known each other since November 2014, but we weren't a couple until November 2015. Then two short months after making it official we got in the accident and after the chaos of the accident and hospital stay, we were living together. He was discharged from the hospital on Feb. 1, 2016—just a few days after the accident—but I was still there left in a coma from the accident. Doctors warned him and my family I may not live and even if I did wake up, I may not remember who they were. But that didn't scare Jeremy away; he never strayed from me and came to visit me in the hospital every day. Every day, I lay there lifeless with machines keeping me alive, unable to give him or my family any hope.

From January 30 to June 18, I spent my time in four different hospitals, with an emergency trip back to the original ICU I was in to perform an emergency surgery on my skull to repair the leak I had. It wasn't until May that I remember waking up. That means that for more than three months, my family, my friends, and Jeremy had no signs that I was going to wake up—for more than three months I appeared to be brain-dead. From May 18, 2016, until the date I was discharged from the hospital, Jeremy spent EVERY. SINGLE. NIGHT with me in my hospital bed. Jeremy was my one familiarity in a world of unknown chaos. In a world of uncertainty and fear, he was my comfort. I, along with many others, look at his strong devotion in awe. I was nothing more to him than a new girlfriend at the time. He didn't have to stay nor would he be judged if had he moved on with his life after the accident. Yet he refused to leave. He continued to show his relentless hope that I would wake up with his return to my bedside every night for three grueling months.

Once I was out of the hospital, the difficulties came. After I was discharged I no longer had an apartment. My roommate was forced to find a new roommate to take over my $2,000/month rent in downtown Denver. Jeremy moved in with me to help me with the long road of recovery that we knew we had ahead of me. My two worlds, my boyfriend life and family life, which I had intentionally kept separate before, were forced to not only come together but live with one another. As fast as this situation came about in my life, they came clashing together with a bigger bang.

We had the little things to worry about, the stuff everyone deals with when they live with roommates. Issues like one person likes the dishes in the dishwasher this way and the roommate loads them that way. To be specific, my dad has always been very particular and neat. And Jeremy is clean too, so that would make for a good match, right?! Ha! Not so much. Jeremy likes his bacon (like every other guy) but my dad *expects* his kitchen to be *spotless*. Ever since we were kids, each of us had a different chore to do every night. After dinner and chores were done, the kitchen was "closed," meaning no one was allowed back in to get a snack or anything until the next day. We were allowed to get a glass of water, but water only. No milk or juice or anything that could make a mess. Anyway, Jeremy would make bacon and naturally, there would be grease spots from the grease splattering. Apparently, Jeremy's cleaning wasn't up to my dad's standards, and the bacon grease was just the first issue that came up. My mom told me, "Your dad mentioned to me how there's bacon grease on the stove. Make sure you tell Jeremy to clean each time he makes bacon." So, I had to be sure to tell Jeremy to clean up each time.

Then, one night Jeremy got home from work and the gym a little later, like at 8pm, and had thrown a load of laundry in. The next day when Jeremy was already gone to work, my dad said, "Hey Mol, I'm fixing washer/dryers/dishwashers all day for my job, so I'd really appreciate it if no one did laundry at night. I hear that all day, the last thing I want to do is to come home to it." So I had to go back and tell Jeremy not to do laundry at night. Jeremy also mentioned to my parents that maybe we should be more conscious of my diet. Maybe not so many sweets and incorporating more veggies/fruits into my meals would be beneficial. (He knows the importance diet plays in the body, especially a recovering one like mine.) Well, this must have come off as condescending and criticizing to my parents. They perceived his comment as if he was saying their food wasn't good enough for me.

I quickly found myself in the middle of two competing sides. Each side I LOVE more than anything. I found myself having to explain the other side and relay messages without offending the other. It was a dangerous game of cat and mouse and not a fun one. I had to walk on a very thin tightrope, constantly trying to figure out how to say something so as to not hurt the other's feelings. It was exhausting. That's how I lived EVERY SINGLE MINUTE of EVERY SINGLE DAY. Until *the incident* happened. Ugh, this *stupid, God-forsaken* jersey. That's right...a stupid jersey. My brother's and my relationship suffered a silent game that went on two and a half years. We didn't talk to one another for two and a half years all because of a stupid, $70 jersey.

My brother had gotten Broncos tickets and he was going to take his girlfriend's son with him. A nice boys' night out. A chance for them to bond. Our cousin's husband works for the Broncos so he was able to score them some special meet and greet passes, something that would be special for an eleven-year-old to go and meet some of the players. My brother didn't have any Broncos gear to wear so Jeremy gladly offered his jersey. (Quick side note: I feel it important to say that Jeremy has many Broncos jerseys and he even asked me, "Do you think I'll be ok lending your brother my Peyton Manning jersey? It's not gonna come back with a rip in it or anything, right?" And I answered with a laugh, "Babe, it'll be fine. I'm sure he won't rip it.") Jeremy reluctantly lent him his prized possession: his Peyton Manning jersey. It turns out my brother and his girlfriend's son met a bunch of players at the meet and greet and they didn't have anything to sign for autographs other than the jersey he was wearing. My brother called me after the game, later that night, and explained the situation to me and asked, "Do you think Jeremy will let me keep the jersey?" I told him I would ask but knowing how much Jeremy likes that jersey, probably not. My brother said, "It's not just about the autographs... it's what this night symbolizes to me; a really special experience between me and Julian (the girlfriend's son)." So, again, I said, "I get that...but that jersey means A LOT to Jeremy." I passed the phone to Jeremy and let the two of them talk it out. Jeremy said he couldn't give up the jersey (like expected) and my brother said he wasn't returning it. The two started to yell at each other and angry words were exchanged. The next day, once Jeremy left for work, my mom told me that Jeremy had scared my youngest sister last night so she and my dad "were going to ask Jeremy to leave and move out." Devastated, I texted Jeremy to tell him how angry and sad I was. Jeremy responded trying to calm me down and told me he wouldn't come back home. That was that. I spoke with my youngest sister, because I didn't want her to be frightened of Jeremy. (We never knew who her birth father was and I just felt like she could use a good, older, male role model in her life. Plus, she and Jeremy share the fact that they are both adopted, they both don't know who their dad is. I was hoping Jeremy could help her realize that shouldn't be a fact that holds her back in life.) Anyway, I went to go speak to her about Jeremy and she said, "Mol, I've heard people yell on the phone before. He did not scare me!" So while I was relieved she wasn't scared of him, I was left thinking, *Why would my mom use her as a scapegoat?!* My mom was the adult in the situation, she should've been able to tell another adult she didn't think the living situation was working out.

It had been days since the incident happened and Jeremy still didn't have his jersey back. I texted my brother and asked if he was ever planning on returning it. He said "Yeah. I'll drop off the jersey at mom's," to which I thought, *Great! We can move on, now.* If only I was that lucky for it to be so easy. Jeremy knew Ian would try and return another jersey and not his jersey and that wasn't ok. That would be like Ian trying to trick Jeremy. This was now a fight based on *principal* for Jeremy but for my brother, it should all be fixed once he returns a jersey back to Jeremy, any jersey. This opened up a new can of worms. I don't even know what happened...all I know is that it is now three-plus years later and Jeremy is still without a jersey. (I wonder how often my brother takes joy in having that jersey...is it hanging in a frame above his fireplace or is it stuffed in one of his moving boxes? Unfortunately, I can only assume it's the latter.)

The tensions between my boyfriend and family were growing but during this all, I tried to keep my relationships between each civil and intact. I kept in mind each of my *personal, individualistic, unique* relationships. My relationship between my mom and me was different from the relationship between my dad and me. Just like the relationship between my brother and me was different from the relationships with each of my parents. I'm a grown woman and have the ability to form many different relationships but I, honestly, don't think my family looked at it that way. If something was wrong in *their* relationship with Jeremy that meant something was wrong in *my relationship* with them. If they were mad at Jeremy, they were mad at Jeremy...and me. If they knew Jeremy was upset with them, that must mean I was upset with them. If I said or did anything that didn't align with their approval—that was Jeremy just chirping in my ear *convincing* me they were the devil and out to get me. It was completely unfair to hold me accountable for their relationship with Jeremy and beyond that, to have it account for issues in *my* relationship with them. What I've self-discovered, is that I lost my identity in the accident. I was no longer Molei, the do-gooder, rule-follower, older sister of the household. I was the older sister who got in a bad accident and almost died. I was the older sister with a TBI and unable to think on my own or form my own relationships. It's been four years since the accident, and I have been fighting a battle to try and gain back my own identity with each of my family members. Early on it was a lot harder for me to establish my own identity, apart from Jeremy's, to my friends and family, but I think it's slowly becoming more apparent that time isn't the only thing to contribute this growth; it's a lot of effort. I've put effort into it and I've had to make conscious choices to try and get the relationships back.

Once Jeremy was kicked out of my parents' house, he luckily had friends in Denver who had spare rooms he could live in until he could get his own apartment to rent. He would make the drive out to my parents' house every Friday to pick me up and would drive me back the following Sunday. My weeks became a countdown to Friday and dreading the misery of my drive back. My silence has always been a dead giveaway that something's wrong. So it's no surprise that every Sunday the car rides back to my parents were filled with silence. I'd like to sit here and tell you I soaked up every second of the seventy-two hours I had with Jeremy but I'm too much of a worrier and planner for that to be true. Saturday morning I'd wake up and dread Sunday afternoon's drive back. And it's not as if my living conditions were unlivable at my parent's house; they weren't. It's just—time spent there meant time spent away from Jeremy.

I definitely put an unfair amount of guilt on Jeremy. I would adamantly ask him if I could just move in with him. It's easy for me to look at where I am now and see his denials as unreasonable and mean, but I have to remember the amount of help I still required. I was still in a wheelchair and couldn't do transfers from my wheelchair. This meant I still required help getting from my wheelchair to the toilet anytime I used the bathroom. I didn't even have the balance required to pull my pants down. My mom or Jeremy would have to help me bathe.

When I say I had to relearn everything, I mean *everything*.

Not only did my life get drastically changed but so did Jeremy's. Prior to this, he was a twenty-eight-year-old guy with a budding social life that included happy hours and late nights out with friends. Now his life consisted of wheeling around his girlfriend in a wheelchair and calling restaurants or venues to make sure they were wheelchair friendly or accessible.

After the accident, mine and Jeremy's identities slowly melded into one and I think it was because he chose to be there with me...to be that "someone." He lived with me in the hospitals so every nurse or doctor knew him by name. My friends knew what a constant pillar he was for me to lean on. My family saw and recognized his positive impact he had on my life. Soon Jeremy and I lost the individual "I's" that made an "us."

Everyone just assumed I was fine because I had Jeremy, but the truth is I felt abandoned and alone. Everyone must have justified their turning a blind eye to me because I had my someone, but what everyone didn't know was that we were going through our own relationship problems...just like any other relationship out there. What made our relationship struggles so unique is that I didn't have anyone else to lean on or go to for relationship advice. At the time, I felt as though my family had thought I chose Jeremy over them so I couldn't go to them. My friends were busy with their own lives and, to be honest, probably had enough of the drama that was my life so they weren't even aware that I felt stranded and alone. Essentially, I had no family to turn to, I had no friends to confide in, and I certainly couldn't go to Jeremy with the problems because he was part of my problem. (!) I had no one. It was as if I had fallen in a deep, dark hole and no one even knew I was gone. One day I was at the townhome alone because Jeremy had gone off to work (I wasn't volunteering at this point), and I didn't have any therapies scheduled that day. I hadn't talked to anyone that day because the only reason my cell phone would ring is if there was a clerical error with my insurance at Craig Hospital. I hadn't seen anyone because I had no therapy scheduled that day, so why would I see anyone? The only thing that had an interest of my whereabouts was my dog and that's because he depended on me to let him out or to feed him. My life was nothing. It meant nothing. I had fallen in that hole with no one to notice I was gone. So I decided to take control of one thing in my life: my death. I thought everything else in my life has been out of my control and has left me with this life filled with emptiness; I'll just end it. I went to the room where Jeremy kept his shotgun with the intention of shooting myself. Now a shotgun is a big gun with a long barrel so it wouldn't be as easy as holding a handgun to my head, but I didn't get hung up on specifics. Those are too little of details to mess up my huge decision—one made so fast and carelessly. When I got to the closet it was usually kept in, the same closet I hung my clothes in daily, it wasn't there. The quick break in the deadlock grip suicide had consumed me in allowed me to ask myself, *What the hell are you doing!?* I ran out of the room and searched for my cell phone while tears rushed down my face. I found my cellphone sitting where I left it and I made a call. I didn't even know why I was calling someone or what I was going to say but it was just so automatic. I'm so glad she answered. "Hey Mols! What's up?!" I could see her smile through the cheer in her voice. I was able to say through the tears, "Bayle, I'm not okay. I don't know why I called." She listened to me explain to her my moment of desperation that could have easily been my demise and helped me see how important my life was. What I didn't see at the time was that yes, I had fallen into that deep, dark hole. But it wasn't *me* that was the thing that everyone couldn't see—it was the hole. The hole was only a hole to *me*. It was something I created and of course no one knew I had fallen down it because it wasn't there to them. Bayle was there to pull me back to life only after I reached out for help. I'm so lucky she answered because thinking back on it, I called on a random weekday at a random hour of the day. She was working, like any normal person would be, and easily could have missed the call.

CHAPTER SEVEN- MY GIRLS

One of the most difficult things that came of this accident wasn't relearning to breathe or walk or swallow, it wasn't rebuilding the family relationships damaged amid the accident, it wasn't even any relationship struggles Jeremy and I suffered much like a civilian suffers injuries from the shrapnel from an explosion; it was losing my friendships with my girls. The process of losing them included a lot of tears on my part and a lot of what-ifs. I had to accept that once was, is no longer. I once had a group of girlfriends that were more like sisters to me...no, they were closer than sisters, they were my everything. I grew up with these girls; we shared so many memories together. So many firsts. So many monumental life moments. So many laughs. So many tears. So many pieces of advice. So many shoulders to lean on when I needed help or shoulders to cry on, so many spines to reinforce and back me up, so many laughs and smiles to brighten my day. Not only were they that for me but they allowed me to return the support and care to them. They made me feel like I had a purpose in life; that even if I felt I was good for nothing else, at least I could find solace in being a good friend. Though it's heartbreaking for me to write of our friendships in the past tense, I don't have an ounce of regret when I look back on our times. When I reminisce I only have great, joyous, and fond memories. I'm so grateful that I got to be a part of friendships like that. They will always hold a special place in my heart. I wasn't shy to share with the world my admiration and pride of the friendships. I made it very known that I loved them. In one of my Facebook posts I wrote, "Truthfully, if this had to happen to somebody, I'm glad this happened to me. Because I have such a strong support system carrying me through! It may be ugly now, but we'll get through! I'm so lucky to have friends get me through!" Little did I know, we wouldn't make it through. We *couldn't* have made it through. The accident happened at such a pivotal moment in our lives; many of the girls were getting married or starting a family...they were starting to build their own stories with the friendship in the background...assuming they put the effort forth to rightfully keep the friendships in return. However, I couldn't put the effort forth. It's easy for me to be harsh on myself and just chalk it up to not being a good friend, but that's the simple explanation and it's not accurate. When I dig down deeper and investigate, it's true; I wasn't the friend I once was, the friend the girls were used to—the caring and inquisitive friend who took a genuine caring and involvement in other's lives. I wasn't *involved* in their lives as much because I (quite literally) couldn't be. Both physically and mentally. I couldn't drive so I felt as though I was stuck out at my parents' house away from everyone. I was also healing from a brain injury. My brain was still healing among the other, more obvious, deficits that plagued me. I didn't have the emotional intelligence to care for anyone else's life except for my own. (I can't tell you how much gratitude I hold for my parents and Jeremy for recognizing that and allowing me to heal!) However, I did have enough intelligence to know I wanted to be a better friend. Believe me, I wanted it badly. I was just too busy with rehab things: like learning how to walk so I could rid myself of the wheelchair or learning how to swallow so I could get my feeding tube removed. Now, I know what you're thinking: *Molei, it's not that hard to pick up a phone for a simple call...* but remember, this was before I had my voice back and I had little breath control so talking on the phone was, indeed, hard for me. I couldn't drive and I lived thirty minutes outside of town so I didn't want to ask for friends to come pick me up nor did I expect them to make the trip out of their way to come see me. Even if they would have agreed to come get me, I didn't have the arm dexterity to propel myself in my wheelchair, so I required someone to push me. Just the fact that I now required a wheelchair to get around was a big enough hit to my self-esteem, but then you have to add in all the details of getting in and out of it and then hauling it with you to each location. I thought of it like having a baby. With a baby there's no more quick trips. Running errands is now a whole ordeal of making sure the baby (me, in my head) is safely in the car (I needed help transferring in and out of the car), you have to stow the stroller in the trunk (same with my wheelchair), then unload the stroller (wheelchair in my case) and help move the baby from the car to the stroller (help me get from the car to my wheelchair). On top of this, I had my feeding tube (which I knew how to administer any water or food myself, but still, it's another thing that blatantly pointed out the aftermath of the crash). With such brash and drastic changes I required, it's easy to see how a sense of guilt came over me. I felt guilty for bearing such a burden on the friendship. Because of this guilt, I didn't reach out to friends when I needed them most. I felt being as quiet and nonexistent as I could was better for the friendship.

My friendships have never been something I take for granted. I've always thought our friendship was one that could withstand anything...maybe it was our ability to recognize the dangers of drama and our maturity level each one of us brought to the friendship. Maybe it was the longevity of it, we stayed best friends for twenty years. Maybe it was the honesty shared between all of us. Or maybe it was how I was never ashamed to be myself. But looking back now, I see it couldn't withstand this trauma. And I say that in a matter-of-fact sort of way; I don't have any ill feelings or judgement associated with it. I don't blame any of us. Withstanding a TBI is a major obstacle thrown our way... it's not a little "she said this about me" sort of drama.

Nonetheless, getting through and accepting the rapid decline of my friendships was probably the hardest thing I've ever had to deal with. I spent *many* hours in therapy talking about this and trying to make sense of it... *The impossible is happening: something has become too big for this friendship. What am I doing wrong?* I had to come to the realization that the friendship was over. It ran its course. I had to call a spade a spade. I can't stress how hard that was for me to say...it's still hard for me to say. It was comparable to mourning a death; I was mourning the loss of all my friends.

"Hey Bayle, it's Jessa. Molei was in a bad accident and

is in the ICU at St. Anthony's Hospital. Call me when you get this and I can tell you what I know." That was the voicemail that my roommate woke up to the following morning of my accident. I wanted to hear how it was from someone else's perspective, not being *directly* involved in the accident. After talking to my roommate and one of my best friends, Bayle, about it she told me it was terrifying. She said she wanted to hop in her car and drive to the hospital right away but she had to take her younger cousins home first. She had just hosted a sleepover with her younger cousins who were ages ten and twelve. Once she drove them home, she didn't want to bother my parents at the hospital but she said she couldn't just sit back and do nothing. "I had to see you and figure out how I could be of help to your family." She drove straight to the hospital. Bayle's account is as follows:

> It was still early on so no one knew much. I was told the chance that you were given, which wasn't high, and that's about it. When I arrived at the hospital, I didn't even know what room number you were in. I just had water bottles and a few crossword puzzles to bring to your mom. When I met up with her, she snuck me into your room because visitors weren't allowed. I went to visit Jer in his room which was next door and he was clearly emotionally distraught. He just kept asking about you and saying he loved you.

> The nurses wouldn't allow him to get out of bed so he was on their watch because of his numerous failed attempts. He asked me, "Is she gonna be ok, Bay?" And I didn't know how to answer...all I could say is "I don't

know, Jer. No one knows."

All the girls stepped up and silently, all of a sudden, my support team was in full force. One of the girls started a meal train so people could help provide meals to my parents and my youngest sister. One of the girls' dad was a head honcho at the Hyatt Hotel; their family was able to donate a room there for my mom to stay in, so she could be a close five-minute drive to the hospital rather than the forty-minute commute she had from her house. On my birthday, I was still in a coma in the ICU, so a limited number of people were allowed in my room. Instead of just keeping me in mind on that day, they decided to spend it in the hospital's waiting room. They even took my youngest sister out to the mall and bought her a few things "just to get her mind off of things." Bayle told me they all knew how much Harper meant to me, so Harper was important to them too. A group text was started between them so they could keep each other updated on me. If one person visited me or talked to Jeremy or my mom, they could pass it on to the others through the text.

Once I got to Craig Hospital and I woke up from my coma, I remember Kasey visiting me.

I remember we just sat in my room and visited around a pop-up table. She just filled me in on the last three months like I was away on a work trip, rather than the outlandish truth of me being in a coma. It was so nice to finally feel a sense of normalcy in my strange world filled with unknowns. It must have been relatively soon after I got my catheter out because controlling my bladder was a problem for me. I was rudely reminded of the luxury I once took for granted when we were sitting around the table and Kasey had me laughing so much I peed my pants. Of course I didn't tell her; why submit myself to that embarrassment when I know I'm bound to a wheelchair. No one needs to know besides the nurse who helps me change my underwear. I was dragging out Kasey's visit and dreaded her departure until it came like an unwelcome solicitor.

As I was begrudgingly being wheeled around and taken back to my bed, I asked my nurse if she could help me in the bathroom first. Once we were in the bathroom, I told her that I had an accident, like a child sheepishly confesses to her mommy.

Once I was discharged and living at my parents', one of the girls, Bayle, made the thirty-minute drive, out of her way, to my parents' house to visit me. She did this every night after work. I remember once, she had texted me saying she had a work emergency that was going to keep her there all night and she was apologizing profusely. I assured her there was no need to apologize. I then asked why she came over every night because it's not like I asked her to. Her response: "To keep you from getting lonely." I love Bayle.

Her older sister, Dani, quickly became a close friend of mine as well. There would be days Dani would make the forty-plus-minute drive out to my parents' house to come pick me up just so we could go out and get some ice cream. It would've been easier for her to send a gift card or pick up some ice cream at the grocery store, but she made the effort to come and pick me up. She made the effort to get me out in civilization again. I would've been so grateful had she not used any of her resources but just picked up the telephone to call me, but she went above and beyond (typical of that family). She lent out and offered her friendship. For that, I will be forever grateful. Those sisters are my two very best friends. I can only hope others have friendships like Bayle and Dani.

Those two constantly made their friendship known by calls, texts or even visits, but it's not to say my other friends did nothing. This accident just happened at *the worst* time possible. All my friends were getting married or having babies when my life came to a screeching halt. All of our lives were progressing at the same time; first dates turned to second dates, dating turned into marriages, marriages turned into babies. We were all headed down our own paths when I was not only forced to put the brakes on and come to a complete stop, but I was forced early on in the stages. I just started dating Jeremy; I wasn't close to marriage, let alone the babies part. But their lives kept going, as expected, and I had to just watch them leave me behind. I was relearning how to walk while they were planning a wedding or preparing for a baby. One of the girls, the one I had a special bond with, did me the honor of asking me to be one of her bridesmaids in her wedding. This just reassured to me why she was my *very best* friend, at the time. She was seeing past my disability. She saw me for me. I was still just Molei to her as opposed to "the girl who got in a bad car accident."

This was such a big moment for me but I tried not to make it such a momentous occasion to the outside world. I would go to bed thinking of my "walk" down the aisle. I use quotations around walk because I was still in a wheelchair, but learning how to walk. I decided I wanted to use my walker down the aisle but I would have my wheelchair at the end so I could sit rather than stand during the ceremony. I remember putting a lot of thought into my entrance to dinner: the part in weddings just before dinner, when the DJ introduces the bridal party right before introducing the newly betrothed couple. I was thinking of my entrance I had in a past wedding where the bride's brother and I did a choreographed entrance for fun...I thought, *Crap, I can't walk well so there's no way I can do a cute little dance! What am I gonna do?!* Then one day in physical therapy one of my exercises was pushing someone else in my wheelchair. (I actually pushed Kasey, the bride, in my wheelchair) and I thought...*This is it! I'll push the groomsman as our entrance! Everyone expects me to be in the wheelchair, but this will be a cute surprise.* I even texted Kasey with the idea and she told me she hadn't put much thought into the entrances but she's sure it'll be fine. Time went by and wedding planning progressed. I couldn't be as involved as I wanted to be given my disability but Kasey didn't make it known that it was a disappointment, if it even was a letdown. She even planned a weekend to take me to try on the bridesmaid dress, and she picked me up from Jeremy's house and took me to get fitted.

Once the bridesmaid dresses were purchased, they were delivered to the bride's house where each bridesmaid could pick up her dress and get any alterations needed specifically for her. Kasey had let the bridesmaids know the dresses were at her house and ready to be picked up. She advised us to pick them up at least six weeks before the wedding to allow time for us to try it on and make any alterations needed. I was able to get Jeremy to take me to her house to pick up the dress because it was only a ten-minute drive from his house rather than the thirty-minute drive it was from my parents' house. But when Jeremy and

I went to her house to pick it up, no one was there. Kasey wasn't answering her texts, either, so after waiting about fifteen minutes we decided to leave her house. I explained to my mom how I had tried to get the dress when I was with Jeremy to try and save her the hassle but, unfortunately, it didn't work and now it's going to be more of a drive to get it. My mom said it wouldn't be a problem and she can make time to drive to get it. Days that passed by turned into weeks. I even sent my mom a text that said, "Mom...I've let down Kasey! We HAVE to make time to pick up the dress."Unfortunately, the day we had to pick up the dress never came because Kasey kicked me out of the wedding. She had called me and said she read a blog post of mine where I explained that I'll be working on me, "and me alone!" I wrote that because I was going through other drama in my relationship with Jeremy. I did, in fact, mean it in a way that I don't have time for other people's petty drama but I didn't intend it for Kasey to think her wedding was drama. I did go on to say in the blog how I'm in a best friend's wedding and so I'll fulfill my commitment to her because she means a lot to me.... Kasey read that and took from it that she was more of an obligation to me and being a bridesmaid was more of a required task rather than the honor I really thought of it as. She told me she thought if she truly did mean that much to me, I should *want* to be in her wedding and not feel like I need to be in it for her. She told me she thinks it's best if I'm no longer a bridesmaid. She said that another girl who was close to my size can fit in my dress and she'll just take my spot. I apologized and begged her not to replace me, but her mind was made up. Just like that, I was out of the wedding. It seemed so sudden to me but for her I'm sure the fact that

I still hadn't picked up the dress just proved my lack of responsibility as a bridesmaid. It didn't matter that I had to coordinate between my schedule, Jeremy's schedule, my mom's schedule *and* her schedule to get the dress, my attempts to do so came off as lagging to her. I hate to admit this but I can't help but wonder if me being in a wheelchair had something to do with it. She must've not wanted the eyesore in her pictures. Or maybe she thought I would take away from the attention meant for the bride. Maybe she saw my walking down the aisle more of a momentous walk than her walk. No one's walk should be more momentous than the brides on her own wedding day. I honestly don't know; those are what I'm left with to think about because she's politely declined every time I've suggested a meetup. I've never had to guess what was on her mind before; we had a relationship that if anything was bothering us, we could bring it up, honestly, and squash any potential drama. Being kicked out of her wedding brought feelings of shame, embarrassment and confusion. I still went to her wedding and watched in the crowd but I couldn't stay for the reception. I wasn't in much of a party/dancing kind of mood. I discretely made my exit, being sure not to make a scene.

Kasey's wedding is just one instance, the biggest instance in my opinion, that contributed to the deteriorating friendship. The girls weren't 100% sold on Jeremy yet. I mean, we had just recently made it official so he still had to, rightfully so, earn their respect and trust. Like I said, we were a solid group of girlfriends...that means any boy trying to date one of us better be ready to rise to the expectations of every other girl. They had no qualms with Jeremy,as far as I know, but it's not like we were married so he hadn't yet established his permanence in my life. Usually, a guy gets time to build trust with the group of girlfriends to prove he's worthy enough. But in Jeremy's case he didn't get much time. Now, remember we had been dating for about a year before making it official so it's not like he was a stranger, but compared to some of the relationships which consisted of years, marriages, and even some babies, our relationship was so new Jeremy may as well have been a stranger. Point being: Jeremy didn't have the girls' undoubted support like I did. That meant any time my mom ran into one of the girls and mentioned a small complaint she had with Jeremy living with her, that's the only impression they had of Jeremy. A specific example I'm speaking to is one time my mom ran into one of the girls at a store. My mom came home and said, "I saw Mallory at the store!" I replied with "Oh, what a pleasant surprise! How was she? Did she look good? Was she with her husband or kids?" My mom told me a bit more of their encounter but held back from any specifics and I assumed nothing must've been important enough to share with me. Life carried on as normal (as *normal* as possible for me) and Mallory wrote to me that:

Honestly, for me it's just that I can't deal with all the drama. I can't keep up with it. I don't like to be involved in it. Never have. I couldn't keep up with who said what and who did what. It was mentally draining for me. Which is why I removed myself from the situation..."

When I asked her what she was talking about, "Who's saying anything to you?" She told me how just the other day, she ran into my mom at the store and she mentioned a few grievances with Jeremy. After hearing that, I don't blame the girls withdrawing from me or my drama. It was yet another thing in my life that I couldn't control. I can't control any words spoken about me, better yet, I can't control people associating me with Jeremy. One way I try and control a situation of someone talking badly about me, is by making all my intentions pure. If I go about life thinking the best of everyone and everything then I'll come off as a nice and good person and my actions will be well received. If I did hear of anyone talking badly about me, I would address them at our next encounter so I could clear the air, or I would *kill 'em with kindness*. But the problem was that I didn't have any encounters with the girls. I couldn't *kill 'em with kindness* because I was stuck at my parents' house.

There were numerous events that I missed because of my disability. Not saying the girls discriminated against me because I was now disabled, but I just physically couldn't do the things they were doing. For example, I was supposed to be a maid of honor in one of the girl's destination wedding. I was in a coma so there was no way I could catch a flight to Mexico. There were a few bachelorette parties in different states I couldn't attend because I couldn't travel alone yet. I had to miss my college roommate's wedding in Mississippi. The gap between us was slowly growing, pushing us farther apart, and there was little I could do to stop it. It was beyond my control and accepting that was a struggle in itself.

There were multiple occasions I would try a new strategy that I convinced myself would fix this kink in our friendship. If I just sent them a Facebook message telling them I'll always be there for them and professing my love to them, surely that would work. How could that hurt the situation? Nothing could go wrong. I spent the next month in therapy obsessing over how to word this letter with my therapist. I brought printed copies of it discussing whether I felt it was a good idea to include "instance A" or "instance B"...or maybe I include them both? If I include this sentence does it make me come off as too needy? (That's the last thing I wanted...I thought I was already needy enough while I was in the hospital.) As I was constructing this message to send the girls I thought I'd send the same letter to each, individual girl as opposed to sending it in a group to try and take any pressure off of responding. I didn't want to accidentally force them to do anything they didn't want to. Well, it turns out once I sent it, the method was wrong. One of the responses I got was, "I don't see why you felt you needed to send a Facebook message instead of texting us...you have each of our numbers." (I sent a Facebook message because I could use my keyboard which I'm better at than using the tiny keyboard on my phone.) I also got a response that me saying, "I'll always be here for you," came off as me thinking too highly of myself. Upon hearing the responses to my miserably failed attempt to save the relationship, I thought, *CRAP! That did not go as planned. That was supposed to fix the situation, not add to it!* Time went on and I convinced myself of a new solution, I'll send a new message explaining how the last message came off wrong and I still want to let everyone know I want to make this better. I learned my lesson from the last message-fiasco so I texted a new message rather than Facebook messaging because, apparently, Facebook means you don't care as much. After I sent that message I found myself anxiously waiting for my phone to buzz to notify me of a text from one of the girls.

My parents live out in the 'boonies' with very spotty cell phone service...if you're lucky enough to get any at all (that's also one of the reasons I sent a Facebook message the first time), so I was sure to place my phone on the corner atop the stairwell, a spot I found gets cell phone service from my years growing up there. There's no way you could have a conversation by phone with the phone being in that spot, but you get enough service to receive and send texts. I placed it there and waited for my phone to beep with each text that rolled in. But it sat there silently. I kept checking to see if maybe I accidentally turned the phone off, but I didn't. If my phone did buzz letting me know I got a text, I would be annoyed at the person who did text me (Jeremy or Craig Hospital) because it wasn't a message from my girls. I had apparently gotten my hopes up for no responses, but not to worry. I had another effort brewing in my mind. I would plan a get together and invite the girls to a coffee house so we could catch up. (I would beg and bribe a family member for a ride into town or I'd find a coffee shop close to Craig Hospital and get my medical rides to take me there which would be closer than if I were at my parents' house). I thought I'd start with inviting one girl and I can just grow the invites from there. My thinking was that one was more likely to join if she knew she wasn't the only one going. I just had to think who is most likely to commit to start with.

The problem? The very first girl I tried to start this with, to get the ball rolling, she quickly declined. I got my hopes up just as high as the last time but felt I fell harder and farther this time. My therapist helped me see that keeping my hopes up and getting them so high was harmful. I couldn't keep living a life just hoping that it would get better tomorrow. I was living a life that, in my mind, once I figured out my girlfriend situation, *then* I could start living...*then* things will start to get better; once that went back to normal everything else will follow. My life would just sort of fall back into place, but what I can see now is by holding onto that idea of my life just going back to normal, I wasn't taking in the present. I was missing out on my current friendships. I wasn't living for *now*...I was hoping that tomorrow would bring back yesterday. It took a death-defying trauma and a lot of self-reflection for me to realize tomorrow isn't guaranteed... why wait to start living when you can live right now? I was gifted with a new outlook on life: live the best life *right now*...not tomorrow, not a week from today...now! I stopped trying to fix the old friendships and waiting for the results I naively anticipated and started putting an effort in and paying respect towards the friendships I had right in front of me.

Some were friendships I've had since childhood; others were new friendships made after the accident and some were formed through my relationship with Jeremy.

One friendship that was deserving of the effort was my childhood best friend. Danni is my first friend I ever made. She lived in the house next door to me and her older sister is the same age as my older sister, so they were best friends while Danni and I were best friends. We went to different elementary and middle schools, though. She went to a charter school while I went to the public school right behind our houses. However, we went to the same high school, though she's a year older than me which put her in a different class. It was those reasons that made it easy for us to keep our own lives that consisted of different groups of friends while keeping each other as good friends. It's like Danni found out I was in the accident and there wasn't a question of reaching out and offering her friendship to pick up right where we left off. It didn't matter we weren't as close for years, or we weren't having our weekly hang out sessions. She was just there for me. No questions asked. She would take me out to brunches with her, we'd go to the pool together, she even set up a time I came in and talked to the entire fourth grade at the elementary school she taught at.

Some friendships didn't have the history like the one Danni and I shared but they were new friendships I made through my connections at Craig Hospital, like Carolyn. Like I mentioned before, Carolyn is a girl I met when I went and spoke to a graduate class full of soon-to-be occupational therapists at Colorado State University. She had her clinical rotation at Craig Hospital and moved to Denver once she got a job offer at Craig. We soon had happy hour dates and dinners. Other new friendships grew from Jeremy's established friendships. Jeremy has a close group of guy friends, so I not only gained a group of eight-plus guys but their girlfriends became my friends as well. That group of friends, both guys and girls, are some of the most kind, supportive, and generous people. With all these examples, both existing friendships and new, I don't think each individual realizes just how much their friendships mean to me. I was in a time in my life where close to all my friendships were crumbling before my very eyes and I was terrified of a life without friends. My world was getting darker by the minute but each of them held a tiny flame so I could see the light. The friendships didn't even have to be ones where I saw or communicated with them daily; heck! I don't talk to anyone daily (except Jeremy...and that's because we live together). I could go on for pages with all the great friends I have in my life but I'll write them their own personal letters. My purpose in showing specific examples is to point out all the opportunities for friendships budding around me. I just needed to focus and put my energy into the ones that showed me possibilities of flourishing rather than the dead ends I was continually being disappointed by.

CHAPTER EIGHT- GUARDIANSHIP VS. CONSERVATORSHIP

What is a conservator? If someone were to ask me that before the accident, I would've had no clue. I still don't know what the legal, official definition is, but I know it's someone that holds your financial rights and responsibilities. Conservatorship usually never comes up in the case of an educated, mentally healthy individual. Like myself, before the accident of course. The accident completely screwed that all up. I obviously couldn't handle any of my financials, what with being in a coma and all, thus, like anyone in that situation, I needed someone to take over my rights for me; I needed a conservator. There are court-appointed conservators; people that do this for a living, or the more common thing to do is for a loved one (parent/child/family member) to take over.

A guardian is a different thing. Guardianship has to do with all your other rights not dealing with finances. *Ya know?...basic civil rights.* You don't earn your guardianship until you're eighteen. Think: can a child sign up for a cellphone service? Even if they find their way to a store, their signature wouldn't mean anything on the contract because on any legal documents you need a guardian's signature. Parents are the legal guardians of their children until the child turns of age (assuming they have no disabilities hindering their cognitive state).

Clearly, being in a coma hindered my cognitive ability, thus putting my conservatorship and my guardianship in desperate need of protection. Luckily, I have a very loving mother that accepted that responsibility without haste or hesitation. The only problem: I don't think she realized what a huge responsibility that would be. So began my four-year nightmare; my uphill battle to gain back my rights, both civil and financial.

The first of my legal headaches was my probate case. After waking up from my coma the terms 'guardianship' and 'conservatorship' never even came up when talking to my mom. We NEVER talked about it. One day, after a home therapy session, when my mom was talking about my schedule with my home therapists, she was talking to them about my appointments and how I can go on a winter-long hiatus because the weather was going to be getting snowy and we live so far out of town. When I heard that I immediately thought, *What the hell*?! *NNOO! I mean, I know the weather can be a bitch but we all live in Colorado. Life still goes on. People still go to work!* I couldn't use the weather as an excuse not to go to school when I was younger...I sure as hell am not going to use it now for therapy. Later in the session, when it was just me and the therapist, I told the therapist how I didn't want to go on a hiatus and she told me there's not much she could do because my mom was my legal guardian. That's when an alarm went off in my head. I just knew, then and there, I had to get my guardianship and conservatorship back. If

I wanted to live a life of my own, I had to have rights of my own. I brought it up to my mom and she seemed to agree but only if a doctor said my brain was healthy enough. So she scheduled a neuro-psych test with my neuropsychologist at Craig. A neuro-psych test is a three to five day test, and you are given tasks and asked questions similar to those in the games *Luminosity* or *Brain Games*. I completed the test and the doctor wrote a report saying I meet "minimal criteria to have decisional capacity back." In our final session where he explained his findings, he told me how he had to word it in that way because he couldn't write that I'll never make financial mistakes going forward in my future. He can't even say that about his own self. When he wrote it like that, I understood his reasoning for the wording. He can't make promises that are out of his control nor would I ever expect that from him. I had no idea what a pain that wording would cause. (But I'll elaborate on that more later.)

I finished the test and time passed but nothing was being done, so I decided to take things into my own hands. I brought up the issue to Jeremy later that night when we spoke on the phone (because at this point he was kicked out of my parents' house), and he said his friend who he was living with had an aunt who was a lawyer and could provide me names of probate lawyers in the Denver area. I was given the name of three or four lawyers so I called and set up a meeting with each of them to see who I wanted to work with. For each of the meetings, I set them up on a weekend so Jeremy could take me. Ultimately, I went with the lawyer I felt would be the least combative with my mom. She would go about getting my guardianship and conservatorship back with my mom and

I on a team *together*, rather than pitting her against me. I wanted to make sure no one—most importantly my mom—saw this as my mom being the villain. We were all a team. Not me versus her or good versus bad. I told my mom I hired a lawyer and she was helping me get my guardianship back, and if my mom didn't object to it, it could be an easy and painless process.

My mom assured me she wouldn't object and, thus, the petition to drop my guardianship was filed as a non-appearance hearing. Meaning, if no one objected then no one would have to go to a courtroom, and it would just be dropped with a judge's signature of approval when it crossed his/her desk. I was beyond excited and thought I was getting my life back. Even if it was slowly, one right at a time, I was getting my life back. First up: my guardianship. Once I had that back I could work on my conservatorship. I can't stress how big this moment was to me—getting my guardianship back. I didn't realize what a privilege it was until I lost it. One day, after an outpatient therapy session at Craig, I was sitting in the waiting area patiently waiting the arrival of my ride. One of my doctors was walking by and said, "Oh Molei...perfect, while you're here I'm going to grab paperwork—I need your signature. It's just regarding medical records; we got a new electronic medical records system and we need signatures from all patients. OH SHOOT! Never mind, you're not your own guardian...I need your mom's signature." As he was turning around in disappointment, I was able to excitedly boast to him, "Not as of Tuesday. Tuesday I'll get my guardianship back!" He acknowledged what an accomplishment this was and told me he would find me on Tuesday to get my signature. I joked and told him I'd happily give him my autograph but I better not find out he went and sold it for millions on eBay. We both chuckled and he went back to his busy schedule. A few days later I went to his office so I could sign the form, and after I signed it he got up from his desk, walked around to me and as he shook my hand, he said, "Welcome back to the world, Molei Wright." His office is right across from the gym where I had my physical therapy appointments and I remember walking that hall in Craig, the same hall I've walked hundreds of times before, but this time it felt a little different. I walked it with my head held slightly higher. When I made it back to the front of the hospital so I could wait for my ride to take me back to my parent's house, I saw I had a voicemail from my lawyer. "Molei, this is Christi. I'm calling to plan our next steps and what happens now that your mother has objected the guardianship termination. I'm sorry this happened, Molei, I am. I thought you said she had no problems with it? Anyway, call me when you get this and we can talk more." I put the phone down in complete shock.

Thoughts were racing through my head, *How is this happening? I asked her if she objected and she said no! She said she wouldn't object as long as a doctor cleared me. I did my part of the rules, now it's her turn. She's not playing by the rules! This isn't fair!!* The feeling of defeat was so heavy and disheartening I didn't know what to do so I just cried. The other patients in the waiting area looked at me with great concern and asked if I was alright and what they could do to help or if they needed to get a doctor. I assured them I was fine and thanked them for the concern. Then my ride pulled up so I grabbed my walker and walked outside to get in the car. I was stewing the forty-

MOLEI WRIGHT

plus minutes it took to get home. Once we pulled into the driveway I said my thank you and got out of the van. I stomped inside, as best I could with a walker, and was ready to unleash the beast of anger that was inside of me onto my mother. I didn't even wait for her to address me with the usual, "Hi honey, how was your day?" I stormed through the door yelling "MMMMOOOMMMM!" She looked at me with eyes of bewilderment and exaggerated her calm response so as to point out the child-like behavior in my hollering.

"Hi, honey. What's going on? Why are you so upset?"

"You objected?! You're still my guardian! What the hell! I asked you and you said you wouldn't object!!!"

"Honey, *IIIII* didn't do anything. My lawyer is the one doing this."

"Well your lawyer works for *you*. If he's going against your wishes you need to fire him and find a different lawyer!"

"Honey, we haven't even gone to court. You're jumping to conclusions, Molei."

I went on to explain to her that we had a *non-appearance hearing*. Meaning, as long as both parties agreed and didn't object, the judge would just sign off on the termination of the guardianship and we wouldn't need to make the trip to the courthouse. After I explained this to her, she told me she would contact her lawyer and tell him to withdraw the objection. Luckily, I didn't have to go back to court regarding my guardianship. Her lawyers must've withdrawn the objection because I don't remember any drama after that...any drama regarding my guardianship, that is. Next up was my conservatorship and there's *plenty* of drama with that.

I used the same probate lawyer that helped me gain my guardianship back because I had built a rapport with her, but if I'm being honest, it's that same rapport that ultimately shackled me in terms of money. She knew my intentions on gaining my guardianship and conservatorship back; now that we accomplished the guardianship all that was left was just the conservatorship. It was made clear to me there was *absolutely no way* a judge would drop the conservatorship, being so soon after my accident, and leave my financial responsibility to myself. She suggested we get it switched out of my mom's hands and into a court-appointed conservator. Someone who does this for a living and a third party who had no emotional attachment to the situation. I made clear my original intentions of having my conservatorship dropped *altogether*, to which she assured me she was aware and working towards that as well, but it was just a process. We first needed to get a professional conservator and *then* we'd work on getting rid of a conservator altogether. So I agreed...we have to walk before we run, right? My mom and I had to go down to the courthouse (on our appointed date, of course, these things aren't dealt with on a walk-in basis) and wait the forty-five minutes for the judge to show up because he was "running behind." We had to sit in front of a judge and across from a complete stranger, my soon-to-be-conservator, and listen to the judge read from a piece of paper my name and my case number. He then stated the request of a change of conservator be switched from my mother to the new lady. The whole process in front of the judge probably took three minutes, and I say it took that long because the judge mispronounced my name, so he heard the origin of my name which probably took up sixty seconds. From that moment forward all my financial rights and privileges were in the hands of a professional conservator, someone who dealt with multiple conservatorships as her job. She added up all my assets and allotted me an amount she could distribute to me monthly. This was all *before* my lawsuit was settled so really it was all my money that I had earned in the twenty-nine years I had lived—which wasn't very much, especially since now the doctors have deemed me unable to work. I could no longer go to work and earn my living. That meant I got a measly $1200 on the first of each month. $600 of that went to Jeremy to pay for rent, because my lawyer said in order to prove to the courts I can handle my money I needed to pay simple responsibilities like rent. He didn't charge me utilities or cable and we switched off weekly for groceries which was about $120 weekly. When you add those in, you're looking at $240 plus I had my phone bill on Jeremy's plan so that was an extra $100. That now accounts for $940 of my monthly $1200 and that's not calculating for any utilities, water, cable, or hygienic purchases like face wash/toothpaste/tampons. I have never been the type of girl to expect the guy to pay on a date so why would I expect Jeremy to share in my financial burdens now? It was nice of him to *only* charge me $600 for rent and leave out any utilities. (My rent I was paying before the accident was $2300 and that's not including what I paid for utilities.)

Another thing I didn't have to account for was my health insurance. Right after the accident that was taken care of by Transamerica, my employer at the time. But it became clear I wasn't returning to work; long-term disability only lasts for so long. Once they dropped me from the company insurance I was on Medicaid (because Medicare doesn't start until two years after your initial disability payments start.) I'm sure I could have looked for a better, more comprehensive health insurance to purchase, but I didn't have the money. I had $260 at my dispense after all my bills. So, state-paid Medicaid was my best and only option.

There were *multiple* months where my conservator forgot to deposit the check so I was left with no money. I had no legal rights to my own money so I never saw what little money I had nor did I see or have access to the disability or social security checks made to me. I was shit-out-of-luck. It's a good thing I had Jeremy as a landlord to sympathize and excuse my late rent checks, unlike what's to be expected from any *normal, usual* landlord. Money and financial rights were a constant battle I found myself grappling with. Money issues are already frustrating enough but add in a TBI and it's a whole new frustration. Anytime I would get upset, let's say about a late monthly stipend, or getting the wrong amount, my frustrations wouldn't be taken seriously because I was just the TBI girl. It was also so incredibly frustrating to be held on such a tight budget. It was embarrassing to have to ask someone else to give me *my own* money. I remember, once, my week for the groceries fell on the first week of the month, so I had plenty of money and justifying my decision to splurge and buy the organic ingredients was easy and obvious to me. But by the third week—my next turn to buy groceries—I had enough to buy groceries but organic was out of the question and I would be left with no money after I purchased them. Then, just like the nuisance it is, my menstrual cycle showed up. This shouldn't have been a surprise to me, I'm a thirty-something-year-old woman who's been getting monthly visits for half my life. The presence wasn't a surprise, but the empty box of tampons was and I had no money for another week. When I asked Jeremy to pick me up some tampons I had to listen to him preach to me the importance of budgeting. I silently nodded in shameful agreement, all the meanwhile, thinking, *Yeah budgeting is important but so are pesticide-free blueberries and I happen to know you agree with me.* Anytime Jeremy and I went out on the weekends, to a show or a concert, I was always doing mental math in my head adding up how much money I spent and figuring out if I could justify it. In my head, I had to put up with the daily headache of having a conservator just until we could prove to a judge I no longer needed a conservator. I thought and understood this stuff just takes time. What I didn't realize was what was going on behind the scenes.

In my mind I had two completely separate law cases: one for my personal injury and one for my probate. I had two lawyers handling the two different situations, so of course they're independent from each other. I was wrong. I haven't spoken to the lawyers about this so I can't say for certain that my theory on the two being relevant is correct, but the more I look back on it, the more it seems to make sense.

I, personally, don't think that the cases were held separate. My conservatorship was held in place until my personal injury case was settled. This meant the judge had a much bigger amount to take into consideration than my measly savings I had accumulated through my life. I remember my probate lawyer brought in another lawyer to work with me that specifically dealt with trusts. We had a meeting with her explaining the differences in types of trusts. (This is where it gets technical and can get boring so bear with me.) There are two types of trusts: an irrevocable trust and a revocable. An irrevocable is much more limiting and basically the settlor—the person who owns the trust—has no say in how money is spent. That's up to the trustee, which must be a professional third-party, usually in the form of a bank. A revocable trust is a much more lenient one where the trustee can be a person of your choosing and the likelihood of getting access to your money is much higher. This is *my personal* explanation of trusts and not the one that was presented to me at the time. I don't know what this new lawyer,the one who Christi brought in, told me or how she explained the differences to me but at the end of the meeting I *thought* I wanted an irrevocable trust. I remember coming home and talking with Jeremy about my meeting, speaking it out loud and hearing it in my own words, I thought, *Hmmmm...that's so weird. Knowing what revocable means I would think **IR**revocable is not something I would want.* So I did some research that night on the internet and came to the conclusion that I *didn't* want an irrevocable trust. My next meeting with the new lawyer was us interviewing a bank to position them to be my trustee. After we met with the team members of the bank, the lawyer asked me, "So what do you think? I think that went well." I told her I think they're nice and I apologized but I told her how I misunderstood her explanation earlier and I don't want my money in an irrevocable trust. She came back in a stern voice and a tone that reminded me of a mother disciplining her child, she said, "Molei, we just talked about the trust in our last meeting. I don't understand what's changed. Is Jeremy the one telling you not to do it?" I was insulted by that question. As if me, the brain-injured individual, can't come up with my own opinions on what to do with *my* money. I snapped back, "NO! This is after doing my own research...like a grown up. I'm sorry but I don't want it!" She frustratingly turned around and said, "Well that's a completely different thing we're dealing with, and to be honest, I don't know if that's an option." She continued walking forward, not making any eye contact with me and purposely avoiding communication with me, almost like a toddler does upon hearing they can't have dessert before eating their vegetables. I remember thinking, *Who's the older adult in this situation? Me or her?* (It was her, she's probably in her sixties.) *She's acting like a child!* Upon hearing my refusal on having an irrevocable trust, she said a meeting with *all* my lawyers would be best. I had a meeting with Dan (my personal injury lawyer), Christi (my probate lawyer), and this new lady that Christi brought in (my trust lawyer), where the new lawyer tried to convince me an irrevocable trust was the way to go. She told me this was a way to protect my money and it'd make it so creditors, family, or friends can't have access to it. I told her I appreciate her looking out for me, but I don't need protecting. I'm a grown woman with a background in finance and I'm confident in my financial knowledge to have my own responsibilities. She came back with the same stern and demeaning tone and put in some scary incidents that could happen. "Your mom could come after you and take your money. Jeremy could come after you. A scammer could take advantage of you," she warned. I remember, specifically, saying ,"You're not going to scare or bully me into this." I remember that specifically because she came back with a strong opinion, almost like she was insulted by my bullying insinuation. I agreed to disagree, and we ended the meeting with her and I being the passionately involved participants while Christi and Dan played more the quiet spectators. She then told me how "the doctor's written report on the neuro-psych exam didn't agree with my confidence." She stressed that it only said I meet "minimum criteria." I argued with her that no one can write that I'll never make a financial mistake. When I look back on it all, now, I see what a double-standard I was put in. One where everything must be so technical and legal (referring to the neuro-psych test) but at the same time it's so subjective (the lawyers and doctors feel the need to protect me). It's only human nature that with time spent together you form an opinion on someone, it's just so unfortunate that the opinion formed of my character was one in need of protecting. After my settlement, I had a court date deciding where the money goes: to me, to my conservator, or to a trust. It was me and my lawyers (all three of them) on one side and my conservator and her lawyers on the other side. This was my one chance to be heard by a judge and to speak on my own behalf. I had one shot to try and convince her (and the world) that I should be seen as the thirty-one-year-old, college-educated, *former financial internal wholesaler*. Not the brain-injured child they saw. I went on the stand and tried my best to explain my knowledge of finances, my knowledge on the markets and, ultimately, how I wanted a say in where *my* money goes. I don't have exact, clear memories of how that day went but at one point of my time in front of the judge, my lawyers asked to speak to me privately in a back room. We went to the back room and the trust lawyer was telling me how the choice of an irrevocable trust wasn't that bad. I was adamant on not having it, but she was just as determined in making sure my money goes to an irrevocable trust. I finally said, "I WISH I WOULD'VE DIED IN THE ACCIDENT! If I have no say in my finances for the rest of my life, then I wish I was dead!" She said "Well, clearly you're not responsible enough to make such heavy decisions. Maybe we just go out and tell the judge that and let her make her decision." At this point I was incredibly frustrated and mad and just wanted to get away from this woman. My head was too heavy from defeat to hold it up for the rest of the time in court. I returned to my table and stared at my lap while the judge read her decision of all my settlement money be paid to an irrevocable trust. She did decide that since I have a bank controlling all of my money there was no need for a conservator. I no longer needed a conservator but I now had a bank controlling all my money. I went from a conservator giving me a monthly stipend, an allowance basically, to a trustee distributing monthly amounts *of my money*. During the car ride home my mom tried to comfort me and stop my crying by saying, "I know that's not what you wanted but maybe in a few years you can get it changed." I said, "No, mom! That's just it!! It's an *irrevocable trust*. There's no changing it as long as I'm living. My life, speaking financially, was just made up for me. I have no say in it going forward."

To say I was dispirited after hearing the judge's decision is downplaying it. I felt as though my hands and feet were shackled and I was thrown in a dungeon. I still feel that way. Living by means of a trust is a horribly belittling and dehumanizing way to live. At least it's that way for anyone who dreams for bigger...someone who refuses to settle. And I'm a dreamer; I will always find a way to work harder and achieve bigger. But having a trust and the bank as a trustee they always say, "Well why do you want more? You can live off of what you're given." (Which, by the way, I want to make it clear that at no point is any payment ever coming from the bank's funds. They are giving me access to *my own* money that was used to fund the trust. Whenever I have to request funds from my trustee they always say, "WE can give you $____" or "WE can't give you $____." I always read that and think, **you're** *not giving me anything. It's* **my** *money. You're just the gatekeeper. Technically, I'm paying you to manage my trust!*) But my thinking was and still is: *it is what it is.* As much as I hate this, hating it is not going to change it. That's my thinking on a lot of things. Hating it is just a sure-fire way to make my outlook miserable, thus guaranteeing any time spent dwelling on the circumstance so bad and depressing it can be unbearable. If I am unhappy enough about something, I have to find a way to do something about it and if I can't find anything I can do I can't spend wasted energy on hating it. I first tried to take the high road. I thought, *My money is locked up regardless of what I want, so it's probably better to get on their side rather than keep them as an enemy for life.* So that's what I did. I went to the bank that would serve as my trustee to meet the people that were going to be making all my financial decisions. Someone is assigned as my portfolio manager so she's responsible for all the investing. I wanted to meet with her so I could talk investments. She's a very nice girl, not too much older than myself, and when I met with her I was hoping to get more of an idea and say in where my money was being invested.

Me: So where are you looking at for investment opportunities? Are you looking at growth or value? International or domestic? Large cap, mid cap or small cap? What stocks are you looking at?

Portfolio manager: Oh, we don't invest in stocks, directly. It's more like a basket of many, like-minded, stocks that all pool their money together. We invest in those.

Me: Mutual funds. You invest in mutual funds.

Portfolio manager: Oh, you know what those are?

Me: I used to sell them so, yes...I know what they are.

That was my first frustrating experience I had with the trust. Them underestimating my financial knowledge and interest in my own money. Many significant moments that followed were less memorable to me because of having to deal with the trust. Like buying a home or a car. Don't get me wrong—I'm unbelievably grateful and fortunate to be in this situation, my life could have ended worse and I could've been left with nothing from the truck company, but it doesn't make this any less of a hassle for me. The trust put a strict spending limit on my house, I can understand that, to a point. If you only have $100 to last you for your life, you better not go and blow $75 of it on a house. But in my case, it was more like they allowed me *cents* to buy a house. And in the crazy Colorado housing market I couldn't find anything. After writing one of my regular emails to them explaining it's just not possible to find a house in Denver with that little money they said "Well, maybe a house isn't in your future. Maybe an apartment is more your style. After all, with an apartment you don't have to deal with lawn care." I wrote back saying a house is *absolutely* in my future. (My boyfriend and I share the lawn mowing responsibility today, *thank you very much*) Another frustration was in my car buying. After finally getting them to allow me to purchase the vehicle I wanted, I needed to get it registered. It's bought under the trust but it has to be registered under my name. It took FOUR separate trips to the DMV, all done on my part, until they could finally register the car. It was all a matter of the DMV needing certain paperwork from the trust—so I was just the little pawn playing liaison between them. I sent an email to my trust after the third rejection saying, "You guys had me sign a lien contract on the car saying the bank holds all rights to it [meaning I can't go sell the car and keep the money for myself] and yet it's all *my* time spent in the DMV trying to get this thing registered. If you expect all the rights to the car you should take the responsibilities." But as quick and easy it was for me to come up with that angry mentality, it also occurs to me "Yeah, but the police officer that pulls me over for not having registration isn't going to let me go with a warning because I tell him '*It's not my fault—it's my trust's*.'" After over six months of having the car, and multiple trips to the DMV, I finally got the car registered.

After realizing this way wasn't working out—the way of me trying to work *with* the trust—I decided I was going to try and fight it. I knew I'd need a more current neuropsychology test done so I started with that. I used a different neuropsychologist this time, one that was suggested by the court. I didn't mind—I was confident that any professional would be able to see my mind was fine. This one was also at Craig Hospital, so it made it nice that I was already familiar with that scene. This test took a total of four or five meetings, each about three hours. In each meeting the doctor made an effort in getting to know me so we would often talk throughout the testing. I came to like this doctor and I'd like to say he liked and respected me in return. He was able to see me as the thirty-three-year-old I was and didn't talk to me like some injured, slow-thinking individual. At the end of our testing he, too, came to the conclusion that I was of sound mind, but he told me he "has a hard time releasing all the money to me." He said he didn't want to see me taken advantage of and me losing my money (since I can't work anymore and therefor can't make a living). He said he would write a report suggesting I don't need the trust but in turn, I need a conservator. When I heard him explain that to me I told him how I had a conservator to begin with and that was no better. I'm literally back at square one. I told him I know that I want FULL rights to my money, and he said he feels too uncomfortable doing that knowing that this will be my life's worth of money. I left that final meeting feeling so disheartened. I wish there was more to this story and a happy ending but there's not. I still live in the shackles of the trust with a measly monthly allowance (one that's less than what I was earning at my job before the accident). But that's not to say I'm not grateful for what I have. I'm just saying I'm not allowed to dream big anymore. I should be happy with the bare minimum—but I'm not happy with the bare minimum—that would mean settling, for me. Not only am I not okay with bare minimum but it's also doing an injustice to my potential and it's not fair. It's like when you were a kid and your mom says you can't have dessert until you eat all your food *including* the vegetables. So you comply to her demands. You eat all your food, even the gross brussels sprouts, only to hear her say, "Oh, sorry, you're a little kid. Dessert is only for grown-ups." You think, *What the heck! THIS ISN'T FAIR!* You gave me a challenge that I accomplished, but yet you're still going to deny me what's mine. I did my part, now do yours. Award-winning journalist Michele Norris recently said on a podcast I listen to, "Don't reach for normal, reach for better."....I reach for better. I strive for better.

CHAPTER NINE-
MY FIRST (AND HOPEFULLY ONLY) PERSONAL INJURY CASE

My other, just as tortuous, legal battle was my personal injury case against the trucking company. As my probate struggle was unfolding, leaving me disappointed and disheartened, my personal injury case was starting to take shape and was scheduled for an upcoming date. My personal injury case is one that was started by my parents upon learning of my accident.

When I was first brought to the first hospital, my parents got a lawyer involved. Their daughter's life depended on the help only available in hospitals and she didn't choose this. They felt as though if someone else put me in this situation, then I shouldn't be held responsible to pay the bill. My older sister was involved in a hit-and-run accident that left her with two broken wrists and the lawyer they used in that case did a remarkable job, so they called him for his help. Dan answered their calls and promised he would help. He started building my case right away. He even made trips to the hospital so my mom wouldn't have to leave my side. It wasn't until I was discharged from the hospital and living at my parents' when I could finally meet with him and talk about the case. I remember we met around my mom's dining room table; my mom sitting at the head of the table, Dan sitting on one side and me sitting in my wheelchair across from him. Dan was talking to my mom and I about what the court date would be like. He was explaining how the jury would be seated in a box to the left of me, and I would be in a seat at the witness stand being asked questions by the defending lawyer hired by the company that the semi-truck driver drove for. I had asked Dan if we could make sure to get a chair that could swivel because I can't move my neck. I can't turn to look at whoever I'm talking to in situations where I'm talking to multiple people in different areas of the room. He told me not to worry and that he'll make sure to accommodate me. I had an upcoming surgery on my vocal cord, that was paralyzed in the process of saving my life, and it was just ten days prior to the scheduled court date. I wasn't sure if I had to wear a neck collar after the surgery but my mom made an off-hand joke and said, "Should we ask the surgeon if Molei can wear the neck brace in court to gain some sympathy points from the jury?" I know my mom was just joking but Dan quickly and firmly came back with, "Under no circum-stances should Molei's recovery be held back because of this case!" He went on to explain how the defense lawyer was going to argue and point out all my progress since the accident as a way to try and prove they shouldn't pay as much. He reaffirmed to me that he *hopes* they try and argue that because it will only reinforce what a "strong and incredible young lady I was." (I put that in quotes, because I promise you those were his words and those aren't just my words bragging about myself.)

Over the next couple of months, it was really just a waiting game on my part...but on my lawyer's part it was a different story. He was busy as ever working away and making sure to make my case as strong as ever. He pulled in another lawyer, Mike, to help him. With that, I got an entirely added team of professionals on the case. Dan and Mike got statements from all my different doctors stating what my diagnosis was and how to fix it (if it could be fixed). They had to total up all my bills from every hospital I had been at which, when everything was said and done, was somewhere around 3.9 million dollars. They hired an accident reconstruction expert to go back to the scene of the incident and rebuild the accident based on factors such as the curve and grade of the road, the tire marks left by the accident and where debris was found.

Though there wasn't much being done on my part for the case, that wasn't to say much wasn't being done. My lawyers were building my case and lining up witnesses for our court date all while the other side was building their case to defend. Since the person suing them (me) wasn't even the driver in this case, the only thing they had left was to go after Jeremy because he was driving. If they could prove it was Jeremy's fault, then they wouldn't have to pay. So that's what they did. They hired personal investigators to follow Jeremy in hopes of catching him in some acts that would help paint him as a bad guy to the jury.

In days that followed, the case became more of an

actual existence rather than the mystical shadow that lurked in the distance. Situations arose where my involvement became more necessary, with depositions being one of those situations. I had deposition prep where I would meet with my lawyers and they would prepare me for any situation that might happen in court. Think of it like a sport. Law is the game, the courthouse is the arena, and the judge is the referee. Only this time, unlike any sport I have ever participated in, points don't determine the winner, the jury determines the winner. It didn't matter how good you were at the sport or in my case, it doesn't matter that I was the victim in the car crash. In the end, it just mattered that the jury liked me. We had to make it clear to them that this wasn't my fault so the truck company holds all liability. All my prep was pretty easy and straight forward. My lawyers just told me what kind of questions the other side would ask and told me to answer honestly. I told them I don't remember anything from the accident; my last memory was from the night before when we went to a concert with a group of friends. Next thing I knew, it was May 18 and I was in the hospital. I told him questioning me for my memories wasn't going to help anyone very much. My lawyers reiterated their advice to just be honest and they reassured me it was alright that I have no memory. My lawyers were pretty confident that the jurors would have no problem finding reasons to like me. I like to think I'm a nice person and I give off decent first impressions, I know I just finished telling you what an antisocial person I was, but court is different. I was the prosecutor, so I wasn't allowed to socialize with the jury beforehand. Although, I did plan on buying them all bagels and coffee but then I thought, *Of course I'm not allowed to do that. People will think I'm baiting the jury!* So I planned to ask if they could just anonymously receive bagels and coffee and not know it was from me. Just tell them the court wanted to provide this to them in appreciation of their time...but my time in court never came.

Jeremy's deposition prep was different from mine. Jeremy also sued the company at fault so he had his own lawyers. He had his own injuries, just like I did, and he had his own medical bills. What people often forget is that Jeremy and I are two, different people. Yes, we were in the same accident and sued the same company but that's it. He had his own experience in this accident and I think it gets overlooked and clumped into mine. That's not fair; it's not fair for him and it's not fair for me. I wasn't present at his deposition prep; they were scheduled to fit his schedule, after all, it was *his* prep. But I can only assume it was no walk in the park. No, I *know* it was no walk in the park. For anyone who has never gone through the horrific experience of a deposition, I want you to understand what an absolutely terrible experience it is. Depositions are meant to get the truth but there's no truth finding. The attorney's goal is to find and point out your flaws in attempt to discredit you. This means *any* flaws even if it had nothing to do with the accident. Recounting the accident for me wasn't as bad because I had no memory; so you could ask me anything you wanted and the answer was simply going to be: "I don't know. I don't remember." But for Jeremy, he does remember. Being honest isn't hard but it's definitely not easy. It's like someone asking you to recount every, little detail of the worst day of your life. In the days that closely followed my introduction back to consciousness, I would ask Jeremy a lot of questions about the accident: "Were the roads icy? Did he see the truck lose control? Did he have that moment of 'oh shit' right before impact?" I finally understood *he* was in this accident too and that I needed to be more conscious of his trauma, that this could bring up bad memories for him. I finally asked him how he was after all this? How was he handling this trauma? Was talking about this hard? He told me yes, of course it's hard. He said, "Molei, I saw you die. Talking about it is like reliving my worst nightmare." I don't ask him about it anymore. I let him know if he needs someone to talk to of course I'm here—but I don't press him on it.

I can't remember if my deposition came first or the semi-truck driver's deposition. Since I was the prosecuting one, I had the option of being present when my lawyers deposed the driver. I accepted this invitation with no hesitation or thought. I wanted to see this man. For how much impact he's had on my life, I didn't even know his name let alone what he looked like. (For legal reasons, we'll just call him Eddie.) The day came and my lawyer picked me up early that morning to take me to his office where he and his team would be questioning Eddie. Eddie was a shorter, pudgy man wearing a red T-shirt. At first, I had the naive curiosity of *I wonder if he knows who I am...* but then I had to shake my brain back to the present day and remember myself in my new life—my life post-accident. Of course he knows who I am. One: he saw me at the accident ,and two: I'm pretty sure my wheelchair is a dead giveaway as to who I am. There's no more fading into the crowd for me—I stick out like a sore thumb. We all sat around a big, oval, oak table in the middle of their office conference room with Eddie sitting at the head of the table. I sat on one side of the oval towards the back. The only person sitting further away from him was the person videotaping so it could be used in court. A translator was introduced to the room because the police report detailing what happened that night said Eddie couldn't give details because he didn't speak English. Naturally, my lawyers thought he couldn't speak English. But the translator was quickly told she could leave upon learning Eddie did, in fact, speak English. Before her departure, it was made apparent that she could stay in the event that Eddie misunderstood a question—there was no trouble in keeping her. But Eddie insisted he did not need a translator. So the translator left and the grueling eight-hour deposition started. I listened with genuine intrigue to listen to how the night all looked from his point of view. I learned he *did* come over to see me once the collision took place, "But I thought she was dead and the driver was pinned in the car so there wasn't much I could do." It's important to note: in depositions, the lawyer asking you questions is asking you *Every. Last. Detail.* It becomes redundant for the person answering the questions and there's also a tone of accusation. You get the feeling that the questions are redundant because they don't believe you're telling the truth. "So you did see her?" "Why did you think she was dead?" "Was the blood gushing out of her mouth or was it just a thin, stream of blood dribbling out?" At one point it got too much for Eddie to keep himself composed and he snapped back to a question with something like, "Listen, I know you don't believe that the brakes didn't work but this is something I've thought about **a lot!**" I was taken back in surprise because I had never seen Dan get angry and yell before but as quickly as he received the shouts he rebutted with his own.

While pointing at me in my wheelchair he instructed Eddie to look at me. "Look at my client! Do you think there's a day...a *moment*...that passes her that she's not forced to think of that day?! Don't you try and get sympathy points from me on how much you think about that day." Eddie got ahold of his composure and said, "Well, do you not think I have my own medical problems I'm dealing with?" Dan held his hand to his chest and offered his apologies. "I'm sorry, I wasn't aware you went to the hospital. What are your medical issues you're dealing with now?" When I heard his response I let out a sigh while thinking, *Oh, C'MON!!* Eddie informed us he's taking medication for...ready? Get this...high cholesterol.(!) I thought, *Here I am having to relearn everything and you're complaining because of a completely preventable and treatable disease...one that has NOTHING to do with the accident.* As annoyed as I was, it was probably a good thing that Eddie requested a break and left the room. I asked to use the restroom and when I came back I saw Eddie sitting outside the conference room crying into his hands. I feel bad for Eddie, I do. I feel bad he chose not to take the mandatory steps in putting chains on the tires. He chose to disregard the law to save a few minutes on his workday, and for that, we're *all* in this situation. We *all* have to live with the consequences.

My deposition was different. It was held in Dan Caplis's conference room which is on the top floor of a nine-story building in an area surrounding the Denver area—so there's no hustle and bustle of the downtown scene and you don't have to worry about parking. In this deposition the subjects changed: Eddie to me. The roles were reversed and the other side would be doing the questioning. My questioning came from their lawyer they had hired, and I can honestly say I don't like him. I have never hated someone and I still, to this day, don't hate anyone, but this guy comes awfully close. We'll call him David. David is an older man, late sixties to early seventies. You're asking, *He's a lawyer, lawyers are rich. Why isn't he retired by now?*

And to that I answer: *Good point. Maybe he's younger but he doesn't look it. Maybe all the years of defending the wrong side and making the poor and innocent look terrible took a toll on him.* He's average in size, with white hair and a white mustache. I honestly can't comment too much on his looks because I didn't take mental note, all I know is that he was *so* mean. He was being a real dick. His job was to paint me and Jeremy like the villains so the jury would make them pay little, if nothing, to me. In doing so he got my college transcripts and tried to prove my "C" in pathophysiology was really a sign of my laziness rather than the fact that it was a difficult course. I remember that moment so clearly, as he threw the transcript in front of me.

David: Now, look at the grade next to path...patho... patho-SCI-cology. (It's pronounced patho-FIS-iology.)

Me: (no response)

David: Is it safe to say you were "checked out" of school? (He held his hands up around his face and used his fingers to form quotation marks when he said the words checked out.)

Me: First of all, the grade you're referring to is the one I earned in patho-PHYS-iology. And second of all, no! Not in the least bit. I got a "C" because it's a hard class. I challenge you to take it and try to get a better grade.

He also threw a piece of paper in front of me titling it exhibit twenty-something. I looked at it in great confusion. We agreed we were looking at the same 'piece of evidence' and he went on to explain to me it was Jeremy's driving record. I was looking at a list of speeding tickets Jeremy had obtained in his driving history. David pointed to a specific one dated 2012 and asked me about it. I answered honestly and frankly.

David: Can you tell me about this citation? Why was he driving seventeen miles over the speed limit?
Me: Well, like I answered in a previous question, I met Jeremy sometime in 2014. This happened before I met him, so you'd have to ask him if you're looking for details.

David went on to ask me questions, trying to make me look bad, but he didn't have much to work with. I'm not trying to make myself look like a saint or anything, it's just—I did nothing wrong in this case. I wasn't hiding anything. He could ask me anything and I was going to answer honestly, and I was going to be frank about it. Meaning, he could ask me about my grades and I'll answer honestly, but I'm going to make it clear why whatever he brings up has nothing to do with the accident. David was grasping for straws. He showed me a video of one of Jeremy's previous professional MMA fights, questioning

Jeremy's personality. I'm sure he wanted the jury to see Jeremy as an aggressive, fighting type of guy, but I answered honestly and told him MMA is a sport. I told him it was unfair to judge someone based on a sport they're involved in. I asked him if he thinks all football players are violent because they tackle? David tried to make it look like I spent my money irresponsibly and therefor shouldn't be awarded any amount of money. He pulled out recent bank statements of mine and wanted me to explain them but I think he forgot I had no control over my money. I had a conservator, so any spending was not done on my part. He pointed to a $1500 charge on essential oils and said,

David: $1500 seems like a little much for essential oils...wouldn't you agree?

Me: you're right it does seem like a lot, but my mom sells essential oils so I'm sure it was an order fulfilling the orders she has.

David: So you had to make the fulfillment?

Me: No, my mom's my conservator. All of these purchases listed on the bank statement were not done by me. I have no financial rights; I don't even have access to my bank statements.

David had no further questions for me regarding the bank statements. At that point my lawyers had asked for a quick break to grab water and go to the bathroom because it had been three and a half straight hours of questioning. When I got up to stretch my legs I thought to myself, *Ok, this isn't so bad. So far just boring questions and stupid ones. The toughest part will be giving this guy the benefit of the doubt in his attempts at finding my flaws.* He was playing easy, though; lobbing softballs to me to warm me up. When I came back David would start to play dirty. He had subpoenaed my therapist and got all of his office notes to question me. That's like using someone's diary against them...and I told him that at one point in the questioning.

David: It looks like in June of 2017 there's an incident where Jeremy upset you.

Me: Yeah, we're a realistic couple. That's what couple's do: they disagree.

David: Well he seemed to upset you enough to where you felt the need to share it in therapy.

Me: Yes, it's not like I went out spreading gossip about Jeremy. I took it to my therapist...what I thought (before this) was a safe space. I'm not ashamed for being in therapy—for making my mental health a priority.

(David said the next piece with his palms wide open and near his face as if showing me he has no fault.)

David: Molei, I'm just reading things off the paper. I'm just doing my job. I'm not harassing you or judging you.

What I *wanted* to say but didn't because I wanted to

keep my cool in my deposition: *Yeah, you're reading the words on the paper that you MADE my doctor give up. You're airing out all my dirty laundry—and it's not even dirty laundry...you're airing out my negative thoughts!* But, of course, I didn't say that. That's what he wanted; he wanted to frazzle me and make me look bad. He continued,

David: Okay, so now that we have that clear—that I'm just reading what's on the paper—who's Martha?

Martha was an issue in me and Jeremy's relationship. If our life was a movie, Martha played the temptress. I was aware of Martha, and Jeremy and I were already working on problems in our relationship *because* of her. We were in couples therapy together because we decided we wanted to work on our relationship...together. I was aware of her but, at the time, everything was still so fresh for me. I hadn't had the time to sit with the idea of Martha and really accept the facts which are that I love Jeremy—and what we have between us—way too much for a *stupid Martha* to get in between us.

David: I'll ask again, do you know who Martha is?

Me: Yes, she's some lady that likes Jeremy.

David: How do you know she likes him? Does she send him gifts?

If looks could kill, the glare I was giving David would leave him in desperate need of an ambulance. In my head I'm saying, *What the hell kinda question is that?!* All the while picturing Jeremy getting presents in the mail from his admirer—it's 2018! Who still uses snail mail?? But I've never been good at expressing what I feel, especially in moments of anger, so I just got very quiet.

Me: (no response)

David: Molei, how do you know she likes him?

Me: I haven't spoken to her so I guess I don't know if she likes him.

David: Well why would you say that? How do you know? Was there text messages or phone calls that led you to believe this?

At this point tears were streaming down my face and I couldn't answer as I was looking down in shame. My memories of the rest of the deposition aren't too clear because, at the time—at that exact moment—my world was spinning out of control. I was flooded with my memories of a previous incident between Jeremy and I involving a text message sent to Jeremy from Martha. Jeremy was busy doing house renovations in his townhome when he heard his phone ding in the adjacent room telling him he had a text, so he yelled to me in the other room, "Hey babe, can you check my phone? That's probably Kyle telling us where brunch is!" I was in the room deciding what to wear so I kindly obliged. I opened up his phone expecting to see a message from Kyle telling us where to go but instead it was a text from a Martha and it read, "Just thinking of you" followed by a winky-face emoji. So of course, I'm thinking,

Who the FUCK is Martha?! Why is she thinking of my boyfriend and sending him texts with winky-face emojis?!? The jealous girlfriend side of me came out and I opened the text thread without thinking. I read texts between the two of them. I read the innocent "how's your day going" text and I read a text regarding a last-minute happy hour that never came to fruition. *Phew! Nothing to be worried about or get worked up over. They haven't even met up. Calm down, Mol.* I thought to myself, 'You're being a jealous girlfriend right now. Compose yourself and get yourself together!' Just as I was calming myself down and reminding myself Jeremy has a life outside of me, I scrolled to a picture that pushed me off my feet and made me collapse to the floor. A naked picture of her, holding the phone above and angled to capture a picture of her naked body. I assume she was about to get in the shower because it was in her bathroom and the tub was behind her. There was a text under it that said "so naked right now " with the same winky-face emoji. It was like someone punched me in the stomach and held a pillow over my face keeping me from getting air. I was trying to gasp for air, but for some reason I couldn't get any. I remember staring at the floor and just trying to focus on one of the thousands of pea-like strands of fabric that make up the carpet.

I heard Jeremy yell for me in the other room, "Mol! Where's brunch?! What'd Kyle decide on?" I couldn't get air in my lungs so I couldn't yell back. He came in the room to ask again only to see me crying in a ball on the floor. Surprised to see me in distress he asked, "What's wrong?! Are you ok?" All I could do was look up at him and ask, "Are we okay?" I then followed that question with, "The text wasn't Kyle, it was Martha and she's thinking of you...who is Martha?" Jeremy sat with me on the floor and held his head down in what looked like disappointment. We continued our conversation and he told me that the other night when he went out with his buddies to a comedy show, he ran into a girl he used to date, and she just came up to him and kissed him. I'm not so naïve nor was I born yesterday, so I asked him, "So what? Babe, did you sleep with her??" And he came back quickly with a "No!" with a conviction so strong as if it was blasphemy for me to ask.

I then asked if she knew about me. "Does she know you have a girlfriend?!" And what he said next irks me to this day. He said, "Yes of course she knows I have a girlfriend. She's prayed for you!" I'm sure he didn't intend for me to take it the way I took it but I heard that as if I should be thankful for her. Like *I* owe *her*. I didn't owe her jack shit and I didn't want to be a reason to excuse any of her misgivings. Did she really think she prayed for me so she can go ahead and screw around with my boyfriend? Did she think she did her good Samaritan act by praying for the comatose girl so now she can do God-knows-what and shamelessly flirt with my boyfriend? NO! *Keep my name out of your prayers!* I asked him if he still wanted to be in this relationship and he assured me he does. So we went forward with our relationship and decided to work at keeping what we have; which included therapy and noticing if someone's upset to *listen*; and not only being willing to own our faults but to consciously try and improve ourselves. I'm not claiming it was easy to deal with the Martha drama. But I'm proud to say that I genuinely hope Martha finds what she's looking for. (I can say that after *years* of this weighing on my mind.) At first it was pure hatred for the woman. I'm not saying now it's all roses and unicorns—I don't, by any means, love the woman—but at first, hatred was the easy response. It was easy for me to criticize and judge, like it is for everyone. It took time to really sit with my emotions and try to have empathy. I realized I, too, had struggled with boys. That was the story of my life before I found Jeremy. Once I could realize that; to find a common ground that I shared with her, I could find sympathy. I hope she can find the self-respect to allow herself to put a high value on her happiness. (Not to sell herself short by filling the voids with making others happy with a naked selfie.)

David clearly knew about the phone incident because he had my therapy notes. David was trying to make me say it out loud...it's diabolical, really, now that I think about it. He wanted me to say Jeremy was the villain in telling our story to the jury, as if my relationship problems had anything to do with the accident. After the texting question my memories of the deposition get fuzzy. Like I'm on a carousel that's spinning out of control and I'm trying to find an image to focus on, but everything is zooming by so fast the images are smudging together making one indistinguishable streak of nonsense. That's my memory of that point forward; an indistinguishable streak of nonsense. I'll refer to the transcript to explain how the deposition ended.

Mr. Caplis [my lawyer]: I want to make a record (of what's happening) What just occurred was an assault. It was an intentional, deliberate, calculated, premeditated emotional assault on a victim. It's the worst thing I've seen in thirty-four years of practicing law. It was a total abuse of process...nothing further along these lines will be tolerated, and—and it—it won't work. Whatever you were trying to achieve is going to backfire, it's going to hurt your client, and it's despicable.

David: Have you got anything else?

Mr. Caplis: Oh, I might.

David: Well, get it out.

Mr. Caplis: I might. I'll get it out on my time in my own way, and we'll get it out in front of a jury.

David: Anything else?

Mr. Caplis: I'll let you know.

David: When are you going to let me know?

Mr. Caplis: Whenever I feel like it.

The deposition continued on with David asking a few questions on my living situation, he asked if I volunteered (which I didn't at the time), and he asked a few questions on my other therapy sessions (physical therapy, speech therapy, and occupational therapy) but nothing else memorable came out of that. After six hours of being questioned about my college grades, Jeremy's driving record, Jeremy's MMA career, my personal life...he decided he had what he needed. I just want to point out, at no time during my six-hour deposition was a question posed relating to the accident. Because if he did, he would have to bring light to the fact that the truck was driving on bald tires. That Eddie chose to keep the chains he had in the bed of the truck—so it's not like Eddie could use the excuse of not having any chains to put on. He did. He had them and just *chose* not to put them on. He would have to bring up the curve of the road and explain that with centripetal force, it makes more sense, based on physics and facts, that the truck slipped into our lane crashing into *us*. It could be brought up that having less weight in his eighteen-wheeler makes it easier for trucks to slide, so his empty bed plays into our story of what actually happened: the truck hit *us* causing the accident. We did not cause the accident.

After some time passed after depositions we had mediation—a time for both sides to sit down and see if we can come up with a solution all sides agree on in attempts to refrain from going to court. Mediation was held at an office building downtown with the plaintiff(s) in one room and the defendant in another. A mediator would serve as a liaison between us. Before mediation began a group of four or five suited up professionals all came into our meeting room to see us. My lawyer informed me they were representatives from the bigger insurance company the truck was insured by. My guess is they wanted to see, for themselves, the girl in the flesh, as if I was a spectacle like the bearded lady in the freak show, the Loch Ness Monster, or Bigfoot. Dan and Jeremy's lawyer introduced us but none of them introduced themselves to us, they just nodded their heads and shook my hand. Mediation was basically a lot of nothing. The first hour or so was just all of us sharing what our weekends looked like. Any good movies any of us recently saw and our current music recommendations were discussed. My lawyer recommended a good soundtrack based on my theatre-going taste. Finally, the mediator came in with the truck company's first offer. I remember upon first entering the room he said something like, "Don't be discouraged because it's not what you're looking for but, remember, this is the start. It's a process! I think we can get there." He then said the offer was starting at 750, for me. They didn't even offer Jeremy anything. My conservator was there because I had no financial rights and she asked in disgust "Thousand?!?! 750 thousand!?" I'm glad she asked it because I was certainly wondering the same thing. I thought, *That's not even a drop in the bucket if we're talking about my four-million-dollar medical bill, and let's not forget: the doctors have said I'll never be able to work again...ever.* I really wish I would've just got up and left with that slap-in-the-face, measly, good-for-nothing-offer. But I didn't, we did tell the mediator to let them know we didn't want to waste our time nor theirs so they should leave and we'd see them in court if they were thinking we can get this settled at a cheap price like that. Another hour or so passed before we got their second offer. This one was a couple hundred thousand higher but still just as disrespectful as the first one. I guess the shock of them lowballing us was no longer present so this one didn't hurt as bad. After hearing this offer my lawyers and I decided we weren't going to come to a mutually respected solution, so we left. Jeremy and his lawyer weren't even given the option to settle because they completely disregarded him. In my mind I thought *on to court we go.* I figured court would give me an excuse to wear my professional work clothes again. I went home and picked out my favorite high-waisted tweed skirt that paired nicely with a silk blouse. I only wore that outfit a couple times to work before because it was my 'dressy' workwear. A silver-lining to this hellish ordeal of mine was that I could wear my favorite "dressy" work outfit.

I was laying out my outfit the night before court when Jeremy came in my room to sit me down and speak. He told me how his lawyer just called him and told him that the other side had found a piece of damning evidence that they planned to use in court. He went on to explain the evidence to me and did his best to deal with my reaction. Then, my cellphone rang and I saw it was my lawyer, Dan. He was calling to ask if I was aware of the information the other side got on Jeremy. I told him Jeremy had literally just told me so I apologized for not being as engaging but I had a lot on my mind. Dan went ahead and told me that the company was willing to settle for a certain amount or else this will come out in court. I told Dan I didn't care if this came out and that I still wanted to go to court. He then said, "Molei, the amount they offered to settle for is a *guaranteed* amount. I know we think we can get more, and you *should* get more, but all it takes is one juror. They just need one juror to not like you or Jeremy. I think this new evidence they have is enough to sway the jury. As your lawyer, it is my job to advise you in legal matters and I can't tell you to pass up a guarantee in hopes for what you deserve especially in light of this evidence." I took the professional's advice, the one I hired and paid for, and I settled. I settled for less than five times the amount that was granted in the mock trials my lawyers held in preparation. They even picked jurors that seemed to favor the other company. In these mock trials they withheld certain evidence helping the other side in hopes of making the other side's defense stronger. I could be present at these trials, but I was behind a two-way mirror in an effort to eliminate any sympathy bias. My lawyers did this in hopes of getting an idea of what court would be like. They even did a worst-case scenario, in picking a jury in favor for the other side and not telling them the most damning evidence we had on the truck company. Even in the worst-case scenario mock trials, the lowest amount the jury awarded me was five times what I settled for. I'm not the type of person to regret. That's not saying I don't do things I wish I hadn't, but I try and use hindsight to my advantage and use those times as learning times. I learn not to replicate mistakes or I learn how to improve myself in hopes to avoid it. But if someone were to ask me if I have any regrets in my life thus far, I have to say settling is my only regret.

CHAPTER TEN-
FAMILIAL HARDSHIPS

This accident put a strain on my relationship with my parents. No, I take that back, it didn't just put a strain on it, it completely tore down the relationship—down to the foundation blocks that we had built other supporting pillars. It required us to build a new one so we could move forward as a family. There are so many things that play into this to make it the mess that it is, but I will try to break it all down and explain it, *from my viewpoint.*

The first and most obvious challenge was with my money. The accident left me in a coma so I was clearly incapacitated and unable to carry on with my financials, so my mom assumed responsibilities and became my conservator. This means I had no legal rights to any money and my mom had legal rights to not only her money but my money as well. I think distinguishing the difference between her money and my money was the biggest problem and the one that most of our problems can be traced back to. No one told her, "You're assuming all of Molei's financials but that doesn't mean her financials are your financials."

I was still employed at the time of the accident and was put on long-term leave. This meant I was still receiving an income and insurance from my job. Albeit it was a smaller income than the $90,000 I was making at that time; I was still getting monthly checks of about three grand, not to mention, I was still getting health insurance. But none of this was evident to me because I had a conservator. Those monthly checks of about $3,000 I never saw because they were being mailed to my conservator: my mom. Money wasn't an issue for me, though. I was focusing on more rudimentary issues like eating or walking or talking. I no longer had to worry about rent or utilities because my parents didn't charge me to live in their house. Bills never crossed my mind except for when they started to become too much of a burden for my mom to handle at which point, I started to see the repercussions. There was a time when my cell phone was turned off due to lack of payment. I still kept my cell phone because I could use it to get on the internet when I was at places that had free WiFi to connect to. I could use it to communicate to people that way, but once I was out of WiFi's reach...I had no way of communicating with the outside world unless it was through direct, face-to-face interaction.

Craig Hospital was one of those places where I could connect to their WiFi and still be in contact with the outside world while I spent my days at the hospital for therapy. One day when I was at therapy things quickly escalated and people got into a panic regarding my whereabouts becauseI had no way to let everyone know I was safe.

I relied on an NEMT to take me to/from therapy each day. NEMTs are systems meant to take people who can't drive to/from their medical appointments. They work through Medicaid/Health insurance so I don't have to pay a fee every time I use them. The fee is paid through my health insurance or Medicaid. Craig is an approved hospital so I could use it for my therapy appointments, however my chiropractor I saw to help me with my scapula problems I obtained from the accident, they didn't take Medicaid; so I had to find another way to get transportation. NEMTs are a necessity for so many people unable to drive but they're also very under-regulated, so much so that they are a terrible danger for many people who depend on them. I had one driver that obviously had never been to Craig and when he pulled up next to a house that was three miles away, he stopped the car, looked at me and said "Ok." I replied with "Ok, what?" He said, "Ok, we're here. Get out." I looked around and said, "No, this is not the hospital. I can't get out." He shoved a piece of paper at me telling me I needed to sign it all while yelling, "I don't get paid enough to deal with this shit! Sign the damn paper and get out of my car!" Looking back on it now, I'm very proud of the way I handled the situation because I often freeze up making it easier for people to bully me. I refused to get out of the car and said, "The hospital's right up that road. I'm in a wheelchair so I can't make it. If you don't want to take me to the hospital then take me back home but I'm not getting out of the car and I'm not signing something saying you took me to my appointment." He ended up driving me the three miles to the hospital and I got out of the car in tears.

Not only is the driver's friendliness or customer service a worry, but timeliness is a whole other problem. I quickly learned time is a loose concept to NEMTs. With each ride I scheduled I just had to accept that time means nothing to them. This meant often being late to appointments, missing them altogether, and waiting hours after my sessions completed for them to show up to take me home—like what happened in the incident I'm talking about. One time, my ride took hours to come pick me up to take me back home to my parents' house.

Knowing my scheduled day, my family grew worried as I hadn't come home yet. Normally, I'd have a cell phone so they could just call me to find out my whereabouts, but my cell phone was turned off because the bill wasn't paid so calling to find out my location was out of the question. My brother decided to drive to the hospital and look for himself. Had he done this about thirty minutes earlier, he would have arrived to see me patiently waiting by the front window where lots of patients awaited their rides. However, my brother must've been walking in the hospital doors as I was driving away in my NEMT on the way back home. When he didn't see me he started to worry. He asked the front desk and they summoned me over the loud-speaker so I would hear it no matter where I was, so long I was in the hospital; but I wasn't in the hospital at that time. Their pages went unanswered. My brother then called the ride company but, again, NEMTs are poorly regulated so the best they could do was tell my brother that I had a scheduled ride some three hours before. My brother was feeling more worried and more helpless as time went by, so he called Jeremy to see if he knew where I was. Jeremy answered and told him he wasn't with me and didn't know where I was but that wasn't good enough for my brother. He couldn't accept that answer so he kept calling Jeremy, relentlessly, at his work. Jeremy told him he was at work and had to go to a meeting soon so he couldn't keep taking his calls. Again, this was not to my brother's standards or liking and instead of halting his calls he doubled down and kept calling Jeremy every time they hung up. When Jeremy stopped answering his calls my brother started leaving nasty messages. Upon the insistent calls Jeremy was getting from my brother, he also got a call from the police saying he was the suspect in a kidnapping. My family had called the police to report me missing and named Jeremy as a suspect. This whole time I was in the car ride home to my parents. This all could've been avoided had I had a cell phone. A major question I ask myself to this day is: why couldn't my phone bill be paid with some of that $3000 that was being sent to me every month? I can ask that now but at the time, I wasn't aware of the monthly checks. I knew I wasn't working so I assumed I had no money coming in. I thought my phone service was shut off because we didn't have enough money to pay the bill. I didn't even think that money was part of the equation when, in reality, money was a part of the equation; it was just a matter of managing my money. That day I calmly returned home and strolled through the front door all while there was a manhunt initiated and concerned posts made on social media announcing my disappearance. I came home to many people asking where I was but what they weren't accustomed to was NEMT's unreliable time frame. To me, waiting for hours is a normal occurrence so that explanation is a reasonable explanation. But to them it seemed unprofessional and ridiculous. They would question, "You have a scheduled ride...how can the ride be three hours late???" That's a good question and it's just one of the many unfair things disabled people are exposed to and must learn to live with.

The monthly payments from my employer only

continued for a certain amount of time before my disability kicked in and I stopped getting paid by my employer. Once this happened my health insurance wasn't just being deducted from my paystubs, rather, I had to pay the company a monthly amount in order to be kept on the insurance plan. That is a responsibility of a conservator— my mom at the time. Monthly bills aren't a strong suit of hers (remember the phone bill), so there was a time when she forgot to pay the company and I was dropped from my health insurance. I used my health insurance *weekly*. Every time I went to Craig for my physical/speech/ occupational therapy I needed to check in with the front so they could scan my insurance. I looked at not having insurance like a death sentence. Luckily, I was able to call my company and beg them to have a little sympathy for me and allow me to make payments in arrears.

Paying my bills is just one thing I can look back on as being troubling in our relationship, but I'd be lying if I said I can't help but question some of her spending. I remember, early on when I was living at my parents and was still using a wheelchair, we had to run an errand. My parents have steps you have to use entering or exiting the house so leaving was a hassle. Not only did we have to get me down the steps but we had to pack the wheelchair in the car.

Suddenly, the simple task of getting in/out of a car turned into a fifteen-minute ordeal. One day, my mom needed to go to the tile store to pick out new tiles for her bathrooms that she was getting updated and she insisted I join. She didn't even frame it as a question of whether I wanted to go; it was just an errand on our to-do list for that day. I remember even saying I didn't want to go and she just said quickly, "C'mon, we gotta get you in the car. We have to hurry so we're not late." On the car ride there I was thinking *Why am I doing this??* I've never liked interior decorating, not even as a child. I was always the least crafty kid of the bunch. I was the tomboy who was more worried about which sport to play that season than playing with my dolls or choosing which fabrics look better. I even played on the roller hockey team as the only girl teammate. To say the least, crafts and interior decorating are not my thing. When we got there, she was pushing me as a guy showed her different samples, and every now and again she'd ask me, "What do you think of this? Do you like this one?" I just nodded as I stayed quiet and thought, *Can we go yet!?* Finally, she was finished looking at tiles and we could start the fifteen-minute process of loading me and my chair back in the car. We got home and nothing more came of the bathrooms between us. People came and updated all four of her bathrooms in her house and life went on. It wasn't until years after the fact that the question dawned on me; Did she drag me along to the tile selection because it was *my money* she was using to update her bathrooms? The thing that really gets me is that out of all those renovations, not one grab bar was added to make the bathrooms more accessible for me. (At the time—so early into my disability—I couldn't have told you things that make a bathroom more accessible, but now—living with my disability for four-plus years—I can tell you having a walk-in shower with a bench and adding some grab bars make it more accessible.)

With just these examples it's obvious to see my wanting to get my conservatorship dropped, but to my family, they saw the act as ungrateful rebellion. My mom was talking to me about a nice thing a neighbor's daughter did for the mother and she said, "What can I say to that, Molei? 'Oh, well my daughter is bringing me to court.'" The only reason I brought her to court is because conservatorship requires you to go to court. I thought, *Believe me! I don't want any of this!*

On top of financial issues pulling my parents and me on different teams, another force that was causing our separation was my devotion to Jeremy. Jeremy has always been a steady source of support for me. I've never looked at our relationship and thought he was the one in power. I've never agreed with the misogynistic stereotype of the man being the breadwinner and the woman doing the cooking and cleaning. I like to think I've always been somewhat progressive in my thoughts towards gender roles. My thinking: they don't exist. (Unless of course you're talking about reproduction, in which case the man provides the sperm while the woman provides the egg.) My point being: that in no instance before the accident did I ever fill the role of the mindless woman who only had opinions that the man has. I think after the accident it was easy for my family to pass any of my opinions that differed from their own as Jeremy's. They thought Jeremy was "brainwashing" me.

Jeremy *saw* my cell phone get turned off or my health insurance be dropped; he saw the dangers that were arising in the hectic finance situation and supported me 100% in my fight getting my rights back. It was this support and help he provided me that gave justification to their claims of brainwashing. So there's one strike against Jeremy: in their heads Jeremy was brain-washing the poor, brain-injured girl making her think her parents are mishandling her money.

Jeremy's second strike was when he chose to live with me in my parent's house.

Remember once I was discharged from the hospital Jeremy and I both lived with my parents. This is a classic case of people-hating-the-roommate situation. Have you ever heard people warn about the dangers of living with someone? They say, "Be careful. It can ruin the relationship and you can end up hating the person." This is *exactly* what happened with my parents and Jeremy. My parents looked at him moving in with them as a favor they gave to him by alleviating rent from his budget, but if you were to ask Jeremy about the situation he'd say he helped *them*. He helped them share the responsibility of taking care of a brain-injured girl and he helped their daughter recover from a traumatic brain injury. They also had the little annoyances everyone can relate to when it comes to roommates. I think it's worth mentioning, because it's more than a little thing, is the state of the house. The only word I can use to give you an accurate idea is hoarding. My parents both have a lot of stuff, but they wouldn't call it hoarding nor have they ever been diagnosed with a hoarding problem. They probably don't appreciate me writing this either, but I'm just being honest. Jeremy, on the other hand, is a clean person. I remember one time, back when we first started dating, him telling me about how his roommate's cords from the cable/Xbox/DVD player were causing him anxiety. So, when Jeremy found himself in a house with rooms nonfunctional because they were filled to the brim with *stuff*, he saw himself in a high-stress environment. My parents didn't like that Jeremy smoked marijuana on the patio. Jeremy didn't like that they kept expired food in the fridge. My parents didn't like him doing laundry when he got home. More time passed by and each party (Jeremy versus my parents) found more annoyances to add to the list. This didn't help my situation in the slightest bit. It was like living in a house of cards and the slightest touch could cause it to come crashing down.

This hostile relationship only added to my struggles in repairing my friendships between my girlfriends. If there was any time my mom happened to run into one of them while out running errands she wouldn't have reason to sing Jeremy's praise. It was quite the opposite, in fact. She'd mention the petty roommate problems like him not cleaning up the bacon grease or him smoking on the patio. She also mentioned to them her conspiracy of brainwashing me.

Either way, painting him a villain made her story more credible. It also gave my siblings someone to point at and attribute blame. Jeremy was now the evil man they could all rally around and scold. Not to mention, they could also join forces and condemn me for sticking by Jeremy's side.I was told that my attempts at getting my rights back were an ungrateful act done to my mom. They would say "After all mom has been through and after she's shown undying support to you...how could you?"

Aside from the Jeremy issues, another ingredient that we can add to this recipe of disaster is my dad's presence throughout my hospital days...or should I say lack thereof. I was in the hospital from January 30 to May 18 and I only have *one* memory of my dad being there. At the last hospital, I had many nurses ask me, "Do you have a dad that's around?" After I assured them I did they would ask if he lived out of state or if he travels for work. To which I answered, "No, he's here. He's just working." It's not that I was visibly distraught by this, though. I wasn't ever left longing for him nor was I overwhelmed with pride and gratitude for his constant presence. It just never occurred to me as a topic to be thought of. It was what it was—I had a dad and he was at home or at work. It was never an issue to me. At times my mom would even bring up the fact that "someone has to be working to provide a living for our family" as if she were defending a question of his whereabouts. But again, **I never questioned his whereabouts.** I understand that someone needs to keep working to provide financial support, however, looking back on it more I see that's not an excuse that's uniquely his. I'm not the only patient that has siblings and a family. Other patients' dads still managed to keep a job *and* visit their kid in the hospital. I don't know this for sure, but I'm sure I wasn't the only patient that was part of a family with multiple problems happening at simultaneous times. My mom and dad are in a committed marriage that includes five kids (equipped with their own dramas and emergencies) and a cancer diagnosis *and* treatment. They're a strong team that's been put through the ringer and have proved they will withstand whatever is thrown their way. To me, that only gives him more of a reason to show up for me. He has a teammate to share the brunt of this trauma with. But maybe that's part of their reason for being so strong; my mom can be the constant, *obviously supportive* presence while my dad can be the financial support in the background. My dad's presence throughout my hospital days is something the both of us have never talked about because its not an issue of ours. Honestly, it seemed more of an issue to defend for my mom. But I'm just rambling now, this is becoming more of my own thoughts that need to be sorted out.

CHAPTER ELEVEN- CHOOSING HAPPINESS

After it's all been said and done, where does this mess of an accident leave me? You've heard much of my past, but I've shared very little about my present. I'm thirty-three years old and about to turn thirty-four in 1.5 months. (But remember, I'll be able to say I'm thirty-three because one of my birthdays doesn't count.) Despite what doctors believed, I am able to live independently in a house that I purchased in September of 2019 with my boyfriend, Jeremy, and together we have done a nice job turning a house into a home. As I currently write this, the world is in the unyielding grip of a pandemic leaving us with lots of fear and even more uncertainty but, *before* 2020 presented its ugliness, I was going to the elementary school nearby to tutor children who had fallen behind in reading. I would go Monday through Thursday for about four hours a day. I would also meet up with friends for a happy hour or to catch a movie back when the world was a place of socializing.

I've got a routine down that I so desperately strived for when I first awoke from my coma: I wake up, make myself my morning cup of tea while I read a book, or sometimes just sit and contemplate the day. Once the caffeine starts coursing through my veins, I begin my daily physical and occupational therapy in my workout room. We have a treadmill, a recumbent stationary bike, and plenty of room for me to do my yoga. Since I still haven't reached the stage where I can run, I use the treadmill to do my daily walking. It's easy to look at where I am today and say, "Oh she's *just* walking..." but "just" doesn't belong there. There's a lot involved in walking, both physically and cognitively; however it's such a basic task and is easily taken for granted. I first had to get a manual treadmill because I thought it would be safer for me in the event that I fell. With a manual treadmill—the conveyor belt stops when your feet stop. If I fell it would still hurt but at least I didn't have a moving conveyor belt to worry about. I walked on that for a good six months until I felt confident enough to buy an electric treadmill. Now, I've progressed to where I can work on walking without using my hands for balance. Honestly, had it not been for the accident, I'd have to stop and think if a treadmill has handlebars to hold onto because I had no reason to use them before—I would simply hop on and start running. I'd have to stop and build a mental image of a treadmill in my mind. *Okay, a conveyor belt? Yes. The front display where you set your speed and incline? Yes, it definitely has that. Sidebars? Does it have those? I guess I've never noticed them...*The answer is yes. Yes it does.

I've had to quickly change all my workout routines and my competitive attitude that accompanied them. Don't get me wrong—I'm still **very** competitive, some may say to a flaw, but I've had to adjust my thinking and attitude. My previous workouts consisted of running on the treadmill where I would strive for a forty-five-minute run. Today,

I'm still working my way up to running because I can't get used to the brief second when my body is in flight—the millisecond when my back foot propels my body forward in the air, simultaneously switching to the front position readying me to land. The other day I celebrated that I walked with no hands for three minutes and twenty-eight seconds before I had to grasp the side bars for balance, saving myself from a fall. I learned I can't compare and set standards to what past-Molei, the Molei before the accident, could do. If I did, I would just be setting myself up for failure; not to say I was so good at everything before, it's just I'm learning the very basics right now. If I wanted to compare my abilities, I should be comparing myself to what four-year-old Molei could do. And I doubt she was walking on a treadmill. Present day-Molei can do just about anything Past-Molei was doing, it just looks different. But different is okay. Does it matter that I need to sit while putting on pants or shoes now? Hey—the end result is still the same—they get put on. (Last I checked, most notice what they look like once they're on you—not how they got there.)

I'm an avid reader and love nothing more than to find myself lost in a book. I've always enjoyed reading. One of my earliest memories was when I was in first or second grade and we had "reading breaks," times when all the kids would sit silently and read to themselves. Before the time was up in one of those reading breaks, I had raised my hand and asked the teacher's assistant if I could pick another book to read. She told me I couldn't because it was too late in the allotted time to start a new book so I should just stick with my current selection. (It was a Hansel and Gretel story.) I told her it wasn't because I didn't like it, rather I had finished it. She had a hard time believing I read my book in its entirety, so she called the teacher over and had me explain to them what happened in the book. I summarized in exhaustive detail, almost rehearsing the book verbatim—page by page—what happened. All through-out high school I was the student that actually *enjoyed* the book assignments. The CliffsNotes website was nowhere to be found in my browsing history because I had no need for it.

Books have always been a joy for me; whether it's the fiction story swooping me away from reality and engulfing my imagination, or the non-fiction book teaching me the science and psychology behind the brain. It could be a thriller that has me wanting to read each proceeding word faster or maybe it's the autobiography of my most recent hero of the time. Regardless of the genre, I'm so glad I was able to find the gift of reading because it has brought me to magical places to get lost in until I pick up the next book to teach me something new or to tell me a different story. However, reading was another thing the accident nearly stripped from me. I sustained diffuse shearing of the brain. This means it was a mess of an injury that wreaked havoc all throughout the brain, it wasn't one pinpoint injury. One of the nerves to my eyes was affected and when I woke up from the coma, I had double vision. The only way to see a single, uniform image was to close one of my eyes. My neuropsychologist noticed I was closing one eye while he was testing me and from that moment forward I was able to get vision help. My care team at Craig gave me glasses that had a prism in it to refract light which helped with my double vision problem. The prism was an immediate fix and very helpful at the time being, but it wasn't a long-term solution...for me, at least. I didn't want to have to wear glasses with a prism to correct my double vision any time I wanted to see a single image rather than the dizzying view of the same object slightly overlapping itself. My occupational therapist taught me different eye exercises that helped stretch the muscles of the eye to help repair the damaged nerve. Luckily, with months of *daily practice* I was able to fix my double vision through eye workouts and tracking exercises. But before the efforts of all my exhausting eye stretches paid off and my double vision went away, Jeremy would read books to me. On nice days, he would pack up my wheelchair in his car and we would go find a park bench to sit on where I could rest my head on his shoulder as he would read to me. Oftentimes it would be a book about the science behind the brain or neuroplasticity and I would gain new ideas that could help me in recovery.[3]

---

[3] I read about a man who sustained a brain injury that took away his ability to walk. He didn't have the luxury of physical therapy to teach him how to walk so he forced himself to relearn. He started by scooting himself around, then he progressed to crawling which eventually turned into walking. The synapses that were destroyed in his brain injury started to slowly form again. I remember when I was inpatient at Craig, a lot of the nurses told me, "If you don't use it...you lose it." Talking, specifically, to me using my left hand because for one reason or another, my left side was significantly impacted causing me not to use it. (If I waved at a nurse, I waved with my right hand. When I went to give a high five or handshake, I used my right hand.) I remember, each night Bayle came to visit me in the hospital she would leave giving me a fist bump. When I held up my right fist, knuckles out waiting for my fist bump, she'd shake her head and urge me to use my left hand. To this day, whenever I have the choice of using my left side, I use it. When I go to twist open the blinds, I use my left hand. When I go to turn on a light switch, I use my left hand. I even bought a book to teach me how to write with my non-dominant hand. I bought it

It wasn't too long before I started seeing progress in my double vision from the eye exercises I did. One of my friends sent me Garth Stein's *The Art of Racing in the Rain* and that was the first book I read, myself, after the accident. I had to use my finger to guide my eyes from one line to the next, but I did it, nonetheless. I imagine I looked like I was reading braille. I read hours on end, day after day, reading and feeling my way through the pages. I don't know if it's because I often found myself comparing myself to situations in that book (*racing cars is often a misunderstood sport just like Jeremy's MMA fighting is misunderstood; the main character is a dog and I LOVE DOGS; there are parental disagreements/problems and I, too, have parental disagreements*; etc.) or if it was just because it was the first book I read post-accident; either way, *The Art of Racing in the Rain* holds a special place in my heart and serves as a memory of this time. It was a gift from my friend, Zee, and is now one of my all-time favorites.

I have always claimed myself as a positive person, despite the uncertainty I possessed, but now I *know,* without question, that I am a positive person. I always find a different way to look at a situation and put a positive spin on it. I can say that with confidence now because, immediately following the accident, shitty situation presented the next shitty situation, one after another, time and time again. I couldn't seem to catch a break. My thinking through it all: *This is life. What can I do to fix it since pitying myself isn't proving to be useful?* One example is with my walking—I can think, *It's not fair! I*

---

with the intention of using it to reteach myself how to write with my dominant side (since I couldn't even do that), but I taught myself to write with both hands so I'm somewhat ambidextrous now.

wanna walk!, OR I can put that energy into hours of physical therapy to teach myself how to walk again. Another example: my prognosis for my employment. I can think, *This sucks! The doctors say I'll never work again so I guess I'll never find fulfillment in my days.* OR I can find other ways to spend my hours of the day, like volunteering. I found a sense of purpose in helping the students I tutored. My driving is another example: I could have thought, *I can't drive myself places anymore and all of the driving services for the disabled community are despicable... this is terrible!* In fact, I *did* think that, but I did more than just think it. I did everything in my power to drive myself so I would no longer depend on those God-awful services. I asked my therapists to help me get back to driving independently and after scrupulous testing I can now drive. My friend situation: I could've focused on just my girls and chosen to stay in the mindset of *No one likes me! I have no friends!* But I didn't...I figured out I was too zoomed in on the girl situation and applied all of their reactions and feelings to *all* of my friends. Once I zoomed out and saw all the other friendships worth putting effort towards, the happy hours and weekend outings started happening. It can even apply it to my family relationships. I could've taken my relationship with my mom as a prime example and thought, *We went from talking multiple times a day and being best friends to resenting each other and not understanding one another's perspective.* But I actively worked on getting our friendship back. I, now, drive to her house every Thursday and spend the day there. We watch the latest TV series we're into or talk about the true crime podcast we're obsessed with. (Shout out to all the fellow Murderinos.) I can keep going with the examples but I'll spare you. Basically, I can complain until I'm blue in the face and think about how much I yearn for things to go back to the way they were, but I'm not going to wake up and find life is magically back to normal. Instead, I go to bed thinking of all the things that I'm grateful for and all the things that went right in my day. And if there are things that didn't go right, what can I do to fix it so I can be grateful for it. Because I imagine a life where you can't find gratitude means there's a lot of room for void. I'll take gratitude. It's hard to be negative while being grateful; not to mention, being negative is miserable. I choose to be positive.

I don't remember there ever being a moment in time, or a specific moment of me choosing to think like this: this being positive and grateful is just how I woke up thinking. I guess I'm lucky because I'm aware I could've woken up very angry. I could've woken up with the mindset that everything's unfair, happiness is a made-up thing and life sucks in which case I wouldn't have any reason to be positive; but I didn't. I believe in happiness. Happiness takes work and effort but it's obtainable as long as you have hope.

I do find myself discovering more nuances as the able-bodied world rears its ugly discriminatory ways against the disabled community. Not to say it's intentional or meant to cause harm, but nevertheless, the nuances are there, leaving a feeling of careless isolation. There have been times when my boyfriend and I went out and the place only has stairs to the entrance. Luckily, at the time, it was nothing that stopped me from going in. I could hold onto something at the bottom of the stairs while Jeremy quickly ran my wheelchair up the couple of stairs until he returned to carry me up the stairs and gently place me back in my wheelchair.

Jeremy is strong enough to do that but had Jeremy not been there, had it been my 4'9" mother, it definitely would have prevented me from entering. Now, of course, I don't have to worry about places that only have stairs because I can walk but I think about accessibility for others all the time because of my experience. I've also noticed how some cities are more accessible or handicapped-friendly. Denver: handicapped friendly. New York City: not so much...or at least the subways are not. When I went to New York City for a vacation I brought my electric scooter because I knew there would be lots of walking entailed. Jeremy and I decided to find a restaurant to eat at and we would take the subway to get there. Because, well, as touristy as it sounds, that's just something you have to do—ride the New York subway. Once the subway pulled up my first dilemma arose—getting on. I don't know if you've noticed but there's about a seven-inch gap from the platform to the subway car. One in which before, when I was able bodied, I'd simply just step over. But as someone who relied on an electric scooter to get around, stepping over a seven-inch distance was out of my cards. As I scrunched my nose and looked up at my boyfriend with worried eyes, I proceeded my way onto the subway car but my front wheel got stuck in the gap and Jeremy had to quickly pull my scooter inside. *Phew! Jeremy to the rescue!* I was on, so the worries of entering could subside, but I knew I had to get off when I arrived at my stop so the worries of exiting started to overwhelm my mind. That time came and I just clenched every muscle in my body, closed my eyes, and gunned it out of there thinking speed would help keep my front wheel from getting stuck. And this time it worked, my front wheel didn't get stuck but I put it on the highest speed and, had anyone been in my path, I definitely would've taken them out. Luckily accidents remain part of my past; I made it off the subway feeling what Evel Knievel must've felt like after pulling off one of his death-defying tricks. Jeremy and I made it off the subway only to find ourselves immediately faced with our next challenge— getting out of the tunnel onto the street. As we were making our way to the street with the crowd of fellow subway-goers, we were suddenly forced to make a dead stop in our tracks because of the stairs. *We were so close— I could see the feet of passersby on the sidewalk just outside!* But they were eye-level with me, meaning all that stood between me and the outside world were stairs. We looked to the side of the stairs and all around us expecting to see a ramp that both of us had overlooked but it was nowhere to be found. Jeremy and I were on a scavenger hunt for a ramp, an elevator...even an escalator would do...but we had no luck. We were stuck inside the subway tunnel, a mere two feet below the ground, putting our eyes level with the sidewalk, but we couldn't make it to the sidewalk because it required use of my legs.

Now I know what you're thinking: *But Molei, you CAN use your legs.* And you're right, I could've left my scooter behind and used the stairs. But that scooter cost me thousands of dollars and I use it whenever I find myself in situations that have lots of walking required (a sporting event, concert, theatre or museum, etc.). Jeremy and I intended for a night out in New York City but we weren't planning for it to cost us thousands of dollars. With that in mind, we only had one other option—get back on the subway.

I was thinking, *But I JUST escaped death by making that monstrous jump getting off the subway. I knew I had to cheat death two more times tonight but I was thinking I'd at least have a meal in my stomach.* Once I made the jump again getting on, we learned from a fellow rider that the subway only has elevators *at certain stops.* In that particular case, the elevator was at a stop two stops away. Now we know for the next time we vacation to The Big City to check the subway stops and plan accordingly. When I look back at this experience, am I mad at New York City and do I expect things to change? NO!! I share this as an example of an inconvenience brought on by my disability. I, now, have more empathy thinking of all the hardships that the disabled have no choice but to learn to live with.

I suppose when I said "discriminatory" earlier I was being a little harsh. I don't think cities are purposefully discriminating like the courts are discriminating against me with my money. One of the main discriminatory things I deal with, on a daily basis, is my cognitive abilities because I have a TBI. I agree with and see the precautions that must be put in place when more serious injuries (like a TBI) are involved rather than a lesser injury (like a broken bone), like the test for getting a driver's license back or the test involved getting my guardianship back. But I did the hard work and took the tests to prove I could have those back. As for my money rights, the judge said (and I quote), "I just *can't* grant you your rights back with the brain injury you sustained." It didn't matter that I took the three-day test that showed the doctor I was capable of writing a check or budgeting a make-believe amount of money for the given expenses. It didn't even matter that the doctors note stated, I "met minimal requirements to have decisional capacity." The matter of the fact stood; I was a TBI survivor. (Side note: my probate lawyers didn't even have confidence in me.) When I was passionately arguing for my rights to her, I said, "I even have a doctor's note! I don't understand! I took the test, you have the doctor's report in your hand, why am I still having to fight for this? I've done my part; now it's your turn to uphold your part of the deal." She responded "Molei! Do you want to know what this doctor's note says?!...it says you meet MINIMAL REQUIREMENTS...that's not that great. It means the doctor still has doubts."

I can understand how some people can take that wording as problematic, but you must consider it from a doctor's point of view. He's not going to write, "Molei will *NEVER* make a financial mistake." Say he did write that and the judge did grant me my rights back, then I go off and gain a bad habit of gambling, subsequently blowing it all; I could go back to that report and use it to sue the doctor to try and gain some money. I could argue, "But the doctor said I'd never make a financial mistake! How was I to know my reckless gambling was a mistake?!"

My doctor even told me, at the end of the three-day test, his results he was going to write. He explained what decisional capacity was and that after the evaluation he found I met requirements set by law. He then read the law that specifically stated: "meets minimum requirements." He went on to be sure I didn't misinterpret his words or take them personally. He wasn't being mean, he was just giving the honest, professional results of his assessment. I'm sure, had the lawyers and judge asked the doctor, he would have explained that to them, but they didn't see the need. The judge and lawyers saw a brain-injured girl and felt they were doing me a favor and a service to the less fortunate. After that judge's decision I wrote her a heartfelt message letting her know the unforeseeable burden of finances she brought onto me by keeping my money locked up in a trust. I don't know if she even got it; I mailed it to the courthouse with attention to her name. My finances are probably the most frustrating outcome however I don't choose to dwell on it. I don't share it for others to commiserate.

I want readers to leave with inspiration and hope after hearing my story. I want them to leave with more determination and the attitude of "never give up." I hope that by showing what a great life I live today, one filled with happiness, gratitude, and a newfound purpose and meaning for life, I can be a living example of what never giving up can bring to you. Use *my* experience, my trauma, as your reason for growth. I experienced post-traumatic growth so just use my story to obtain the positive (growth) without having to withstand the negative (trauma). Regardless of the obstacle you face; just know, there's always a way forward.

ACKNOWLEDGEMENTS

My two book coaches, Amy and Jodie, who were patient, helpful and insightful. They pushed me to be a better writer. My fellow author and writer, Audrey, who not only helped me with editing my book but helped me once I finished writing the manuscript and helped me find a publisher. Julia at Publishizer who was a HUGE support and helped me find my way through the murky waters of the publishing world. An immense amount of credit goes to Priscilla Harding, Kim King (my former boss & co-worker) and Rob (an avid supporter and friend of mine I met through Jeremy) for the huge financial support shown in my campaign. And last but, certainly, not least: to Roger who I found through the scary and overwhelming publishing phase. I found an editor, a mentor and a friend. THANK YOU!

ABOUT
ATMOSPHERE PRESS

Atmosphere Press is an independent, full-service publisher for excellent books in all genres and for all audiences. Learn more about what we do at atmospherepress.com.

We encourage you to check out some of Atmosphere's latest releases, which are available at Amazon.com and via order from your local bookstore:

Out and Back: Essays on a Family in Motion, by Elizabeth Templeman
Just Be Honest, by Cindy Yates
You Crazy Vegan: Coming Out as a Vegan Intuitive, by Jessica Ang
Detour: Lose Your Way, Find Your Path, by S. Mariah Rose
To B&B or Not to B&B: Deromanticizing the Dream, by Sue Marko
Convergence: The Interconnection of Extraordinary Experiences, by Barbara Mango and Lynn Miller
Sacred Fool, by Nathan Dean Talamantez
My Place in the Spiral, by Rebecca Beardsall
My Eight Dads, by Mark Kirby

ABOUT THE AUTHOR

Molei (pronounced Molly) Wright is a TBI (traumatic brain injury) survivor trying to find her purpose and place in this world with this new life she's learning to live. In her memoir, My Way Forward, she elaborates on her experiences as a disabled woman after a horrific car crash nearly left her dead and in a coma for fourteen weeks. Her relentless optimism paired with her new outlook on life allows her to take on each new obstacle thrown her way with unfailing determination. She leaves nothing out; the good, the bad, and the ugly but it ultimately reveals the beauty that lies ahead. She hopes that readers will read her story and gain inspiration from it; to see that no matter how tough it gets, there's always a way.